XHTML

explained

Other Titles of Interest

Titles in italics are by John Shelley

XHTML and CSS

explained

by

John Shelley

BERNARD BABANI (publishing) LTD
THE GRAMPIANS
SHEPHERDS BUSH ROAD
LONDON W6 7NF
ENGLAND

www.babanibooks.com

PLEASE NOTE

Although every care has been taken with the production of this book to ensure that any projects, designs, modifications and/or programs, etc., contained herewith, operate in a correct and safe manner and also that any components specified are normally available in Great Britain, the Publishers and Author(s) do not accept responsibility in any way for the failure (including fault in design) of any project, design, modification or program to work correctly or to cause damage to any equipment that it may be connected to or used in conjunction with, or in respect of any other damage or injury that may be so caused, nor do the Publishers accept responsibility in any way for the failure to obtain specified components.

Notice is also given that if equipment that is still under warranty is modified in any way or used or connected with home-built equipment then that warranty may be void.

© 2001 BERNARD BABANI (publishing) LTD

First Published - March 2001
Reprinted - January 2002

British Library Cataloguing in Publication Data

A catalogue record for this book is available from the British Library

ISBN 0 85934 501 7

Cover Design by Gregor Arthur
Printed and Bound in Great Britain by Guernsey Press

Preface

In this book, we explain how to create and design web pages using the eXtensible Hypertext Markup Language (XHTML) and cascading style sheets (CSS). Ideally, XHTML is used to refer to the content of the page, namely, all the text and images an author wants to include, whereas CSS is used to refer to how the content is to be presented, the presentational aspect.

There is a close relationship between XHTML and XML (the eXtensible Markup Language). This will be discussed since it is not possible to fully understand XHTML without knowing something about XML. As we shall discover, CSS may also be used to present the content of XML documents.

In order to follow and use the examples in this text, you will need:

- Internet Explorer version 5 (IE5)
- any editor or word processor, such as NotePad or Word

Netscape 4.5 or higher may also be used, but it has not yet implemented some of the CSS properties. At the time of writing, December 2000, Netscape 7 is being developed which promises a fuller implementation of CSS. Your readers will also require the latest versions of these browsers in order to correctly display your web pages.

The new breed of Internet access devices, such as palm tops, TV boxes, home telephones, talking car phones, etc., require the new XHTML in order to render information either visually or aurally. The old HTML cannot cope, hence the need to learn XHTML.

Fortunately for those of you who already know HTML, most of its mark-up tags form part of XHTML, but the latter has a much stricter syntax which is rigorously enforced by the new devices.

Although we are in an interim period, where HTML still dominates the Web and where only the latest browsers can support XHTML and CSS, it will not be too long before XML and XHTML take centre stage. Now is the time to become familiar with the future.

The examples have been tested in IE5 and Netscape version 4.5. It was not possible to exhaustively test every property and all of their values. You will need to experiment with those not discussed in this text.

About the Author

John Shelley took his Masters degree in Computing at Imperial College, London, where he has worked as a lecturer in the Centre for Computing Services for some twenty-five years.

He hopes this text will prove useful to those who want to learn XHTML and CSS at a human level.

Trademarks

Microsoft, MS-DOS, Microsoft Windows, Internet Assistant, Internet Explorer, FrontPage, Outlook, Word are registered trademarks of Microsoft Corporation. The clipart used in some illustrations has been taken from the Clipart Gallery of Word 97.

Unix is a registered trademark of AT&T.

JavaScript, AskJeeves, Dreamweaver, Netscape, Opera are registered trademarks or copyrights of their relevant organisations.

References to the various URLs on the Internet are acknowledged here.

All other trademarks are the registered and legally protected trademarks of the companies who make the products. There is no intent to use the trademarks generically and readers should investigate ownership of a trademark before using it for any purpose.

References have been made to the W3C Specification for XHTML and CSS2. The following acknowledgement is duly noted:

For CSS2:
"Copyright (c) 1997 World Wide Web Consortium, (Massachusetts Institute of Technology, Institut National de Recherche en Informatique et en Automatique, Keio University). All Rights Reserved."

For XHTML 1.0:
"Copyright (c)2000 W3C(r) (MIT, INRIA, Keio), All Rights Reserved. W3C liability, trademark, document use and software licensing rules apply."

Contents

Part 1

An Introduction to XHTML

In this section, we shall examine the basics of XHTML:

- the mark-up tags used and the syntax.
- how to create web pages using the XHTML Web language
- empty and non-empty tags
- block and inline elements
- how to create lists
- element attributes
- how to put images into our pages
- summarise the XHTML syntax
- briefly discuss the connection between XML and XHTML

In order to understand what follows, you should:

- be able to use a word processor, even basic Notepad
- have called up web pages via a browser
- know what browsers are, such as Netscape and Internet Explorer (IE)

1: XHTML - an Introduction

I assume that you have already used a browser to find some information over the World Wide Web (WWW). How was that page written? It was written in HTML, but HTML will not be developed any further and a new version has been introduced called the eXtensible Hypertext Mark-up Language - XHTML.

Many books start off with a chapter explaining where XHTML came from, how it relates to HTML, XML and SGML. I found all this too confusing when I was starting out. So we shall discuss these issues in Chapter 21, after you have become familiar with XHTML and CSS (Cascading Style Sheets). Presumably, you are reading this text because you want and need to know how to write XHTML web pages. So why not start right now?

XHTML - the eXtensible Hypertext Mark-up Language

This is a language for creating web pages. It is identical to HTML except that the rules or *syntax* for using the language are far stricter than HTML. If you already know HTML, then you already know 85% of XHTML. All the familiar HTML tags and attributes form part of the new XHTML, except that, in practice, we tend to use fewer of them, relying on style sheets to do our formatting.

Mark-up Language

Mark-up is a publishing term for how text is to be formatted, such as the typeface, the size of the characters, whether the text is bold or italic, its colour and so on. In this text, for example, I use an Arial typeface rather than Times New Roman and a 10.5 point size.

XHTML is more like a text formatter, a type of program which pre-dated our current word processors. With a word processor, as we all know, we type in text and can format the text in, say, italic, change its colour and even the typeface. We *instantly* see the result. With a text formatter, the mark-up codes are typed in alongside the actual text. We do not see what the text looks like until the web page is opened in a browser such as Netscape or Internet Explorer (IE). It is the browser which will read the mark-up codes and then display the text according to these codes. In XHTML, these codes are called *tags* or sometimes *elements*.

Mark-up Tags

Mark-up tags are used to instruct a Web browser how to format the text. Each tag has a unique identifier enclosed in angle brackets - < >. 'b' is a tag identifier telling the browser to begin to display the text in bold. The </b> tells the browser to stop bolding. Thus:

```
Now begin to <b> bold this text. </b> Back to
normal text.
```

would result in a Web browser displaying:

Now begin to **bold this text.** Back to normal text.

See how both the text to be displayed and the mark-up tags are typed together. That is what we mean by XHTML being a text formatter. It is only when it is opened by a browser program that we see exactly how the text will look. What the web author types in, the text and tags, is called the *source code*. The browser reads the source code and then displays the text according to the mark-up tags.

All tag names must be written in lowercase. Case was not significant in HTML but is rigorously enforced in XHTML.

<i> is the tag identifier for *italic* and <u> is the identifier for underline. These and many other tags have two parts, a *start* tag (also called an *opening* tag) and an *end* tag (also

4

called a *closing* tag). The ending tag is the same as the starting tag except that it includes a forward slash - /. Everything between the pair of tags will be displayed by the browser in bold, italic or whatever, and usually in the Times New Roman typeface. For example, the following XHTML source code:

```
The following words are in <b>bold</b> and in
<i>italic</i> and <u>underlined</u>.
```

would be displayed by a Web browser as:

> The following words are in **bold** and in *italic* and underlined.

Empty and Non-empty tags

Some elements have just one tag, for example: `<br/>` and `<hr/>`. The former is known as the *break* tag because it specifies that whatever text *follows* the tag must begin on the next line, whereas, the `<hr/>` causes a horizontal rule (a line) to appear across the width of the screen. These elements are called *empty tags* because they do not contain any text to be formatted. Consequently, they do not require a closing tag. Those tags which do format text are called *non-empty tags*. They are often referred to as *container* tags because they contain text to be formatted in some way. The *start* tag begins the desired format, the *end* tag turns it off.

In XHTML, the tag name *must* be in lowercase. In HTML, case was not an issue. This is one of the ten main differences between the two languages. Another difference is that all tags must be *terminated*. Non-empty tags must have a closing tag:

```
<b>some bold text </b>
```

Empty tags must have a forward slash *after* the tag identifier: `<hr />` and `<br />`.

A Complete XHTML Document

An XHTML document has three parts, a DTD *declaration*, a *head* and a *body*. Do not get depressed about what a DTD declaration means. In Chapter 8, we shall explain its role in detail, for the meantime, simply put these first few lines at the top of all your XHTML web documents.

```
<?xml version="1.0" encoding="UTF-8"?>
<!DOCTYPE html
PUBLIC "-//W3C//DTD XHTML 1.0 Transitional//EN"
       "http://www.w3.org/TR/xhtml1/DTD/
        xhtml1-transitional.dtd">
<html xmlns="http://www.w3.org/1999/xhtml"
       xml:lang="en" lang="en">
```

Like a human being, a Web document must contain only *one* head and *one* body. Different browsers do different things when more than one body tag or head element is met. Some ignore the 'error' and simply carry on, others will become confused and will not display anything which follows a second head or body. As time goes on, browsers will no longer overlook this error and will refuse to display any page with more than one head or body element.

```
<?xml version="1.0" encoding="UTF-8"?>
<!DOCTYPE html
PUBLIC "-//W3C//DTD XHTML 1.0 Transitional//EN"
       "http://www.w3.org/TR/xhtml1/DTD/
        xhtml1-transitional.dtd">
<html xmlns="http://www.w3.org/1999/xhtml"
       xml:lang="en" lang="en">
<head>
<title> Dotheboys Hall - School for young
Gentlemen </title>
</head>
<body>
... Here we enter all the text and images which
we want a browser to display to our readers. ...
</body>
</html>
```

The declaration

1. The first thing to note is that everything in bold looks very similar to a standard HTML document. The first few lines do not and we shall need to examine these in detail in a later chapter. For the moment, all we need to do is to include them in all our examples.

It would be a good idea to create a template and save it to avoid having to type in the declaration each time you begin a new web page.

2. We have an opening `html` tag, also with something new in it which again will be discussed later in Chapter 8.

3. In HTML, the `<html>` ... `</html>` tags were optional, but they are mandatory in XHTML.

4. In XHTML, you may not omit `<head>` and `<body>` elements and the first element in the `<head>` must be a `<title>` element.

We shall now examine each of these elements in detail.

`<html>` ... `</html>` It is a strict requirement in XHTML that the web document be enclosed in the non-empty `<html>` ... `</html>` tags. The opening `<html>` tag must include a reference to the XML namespace, see page 93. For the time being, just include it exactly as shown above.

Some non-empty tags, such as the `<html>...</html>`, `<head>...</head>`, `<body>...</body>` elements do not contain text to be formatted but contain other elements. The `html` tag, for example, must contain a `head` and a `body` element; the `head` tag must contain a `<title>...</title>` element, and so on.

`<head>` ... `</head>` The *head* contains general information about the document, mainly for the benefit of the browser, and is enclosed in the non-empty pair `<head>` ... `</head>`. What is contained in the `<head>` is not

7

displayed on the screen. For the moment we will use the head section to put in a mandatory `<title>` tag and later use it to include our style sheets.

`<title> ... </title>` Many browsers use the text within the `<title>` tags to label the *display window* i.e. the blue title bar at the top of the window in which the Web document is displayed. The text may also appear in the *Favorites* or *Bookmarks* lists should you save the address of that particular page.

It is pointless trying to format (change the typeface, size and colour of) the text within the `<title>` tags, since each browser has its own built-in style for formatting such titles.

Dotheboys Hall - School for young Gentlemen - Microsoft Internet Explorer

File   Edit   View   Favorites   Tools   Help

The `<title>` tags are also used by Web search-engines to collect keywords and add them to their database. These databases are used later to find matches for keywords typed in by users of the search engines. Therefore, the text contained in the `<title>` tags should be short yet sufficient to identify the document's content by use of keywords.

All XHTML documents *must* contain the `<title>` tag and failure to include a `<title>` tag will cause all of the latest browsers to display a blank page!

`<body> ... </body>` The body part, enclosed between the tag-pair `<body> ... </body>`, contains the actual text and images which an author wishes to have displayed when someone calls up his/her Web page.

Exercise 1: Creating a simple Web page
Here is a complete XHTML document. A browser program, such as Netscape, Internet Explorer (IE) or Opera, reads this source code and displays the text according to what

8

mark-up tags have been included by the author of the Web page.

You may use any text editor or word processor to type the source code which includes not only the textual content but also the tags, but the resulting file must be saved as a *text only* file. Personally, I use Word for Windows; many others prefer Notepad.

Call up your editor and type in the following source code. Save the file as *text only* with a name and an `htm` or `html` *extension* in one of the folders on your hard disc. When creating names for your web documents, it is very bad practice to include spaces. `exercise1.htm` is far safer than `exercise 1.htm`.

It would be a good idea to create a new folder specifically for your web files.

Having saved the file, call up your Web browser to see what the document will look like on the Web. In Netscape or IE, this involves choosing *File*, then *Open File*; rummaging around to find the folder and then clicking on the name of the file.

```
<?xml version="1.0" encoding="UTF-8"?>
<!DOCTYPE html
PUBLIC "-//W3C//DTD XHTML 1.0 Transitional//EN"
        "http://www.w3.org/TR/xhtml1/DTD/
         xhtml1-transitional.dtd">
<html xmlns="http://www.w3.org/1999/xhtml"
        xml:lang="en" lang="en">
<head>
<title>First XHTML exercise</title>
</head>
<body>
  <b>Welcome.</b> This is my first XHTML page.
</body>
</html>
```

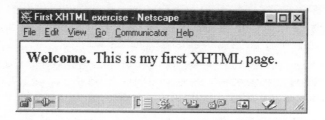

Notes:

1. By opening this file in your local web browser, you can see what the world will see when this Web page is called up over the Internet.

2. Obviously, the actual mark-up tags will not be displayed.

3. When saving your file, you must include the `.htm` extension so that when it is opened by a browser, the extension tells the browser that the file is a Web document and to display it according to your mark-up tags.

4. My source code has been laid out with line breaks so that it is easier for you (and me!) to read. I tend to 'mimic' how it should look on the screen, as far as possible. However, the entire source code could be typed on one long line, indeed, this is effectively how it is received by the browser. It is the tags which then tell the browser how it must be displayed on the computer screen.

5. The entire document consists of:
- the mandatory declaration lines
- the `html` tags to contain the *head* and *body* elements
- the `head` to contain the mandatory *title* tags
- the `body` to contain what we want to display as well as how it must be displayed according to our mark-up tags (we have used only the <b> .. </b> tag)

6. Note how the text contained in the `title` tags appears on the title bar of the browser.

Jargon

empty: refers to a tag which has no ending tag and consequently does not contain or format text.

identifier: a unique letter or group of characters which identifies a formatting style to apply to text, e.g. `<i>` for italics, `<b>` for bold.

non-empty: refers to a tag which has a start and an end tag. The pair contains text or other tags and is, therefore, sometimes called a *container* tag or element.

points: the size of a character. 72 points is an inch. 12 points (frequently written as 12pt) is one-sixth of an inch, the standard size of text in many books. 10pt is commonly used for paperback books. This book has paragraph text in 10.5pt.

source code: a complete file containing both the content and the XHTML tags. The source file is read by a browser and its content displayed as indicated by the XHTML tags.

tags: also called elements. They tell the browser how to mark up the contents of the Web page.

What you have learnt

We have seen how to create a complete Web page using XHTML mark-up tags and how to bold, italicise and underline text.

A Web page can be created in any word processor or text editor but must be saved as a text-only file with a `.htm` extension. It can be saved on your hard disc and opened by your browser program so that you can see how it will look when it is finally stored on your Web server and the world invited to visit your web page. This means that you can create all your Web documents without being connected to an ISP (Internet Service Provider).

An XHTML Web document has three main parts - a *declaration*, a *head* and a *body*. What is placed in the *body* will be displayed by the browser on the computer screen.

11

The *head* provides some basic information for the browser, such as what title to put on the top title bar of the window. we shall discuss other uses later in the book.

2: Basic Mark-up Tags

In this Chapter we shall look at the basic rules or syntax of XHTML and examine some of the more common tags by which we can create the web page shown below. The tags are discussed first, and then combined into the web page below.

What is covered

- `<p>...</p>`
- `<h1>...</h6>`
- `<br/>`
- `<hr/>`
- `<center>...</center>`
- `<blockquote> ... </blockquote>`

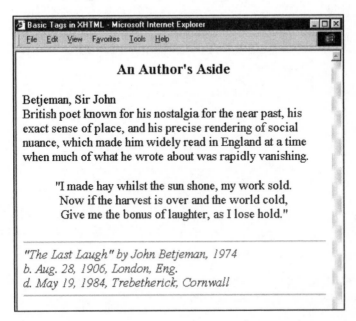

The <p> ... </p> tag

The paragraph tag is used when we have text which requires an automatic line space before and after. Note the use of *lowercase* for the tag identifiers. This is a requirement for *all* tags used in XHTML, they must be in lowercase, never in uppercase.

All XHTML tags *must* have a closing tag. This was an optional feature with some non-empty tags in HTML.

The Heading tags: <h1>...</h1> - <h6>...</h6>

The non-empty <h1>..</h1> tag denotes a Header 1 level. All the text contained between the starting tag <h1> and the closing tag </h1> will be in large, bold characters.

There are six heading levels in all. Figure 2.1 shows examples of each. Note that some headings are in bold and others in italic. Usually, the text is in Times New Roman and a typical point size is also given.

The actual point sizes and typefaces were not defined in the original HTML standard (RFC 1866). The point sizes given were a *suggestion* but today, most browsers display <h1> in 24 points (written as 24pt).

Level	Display format - actual size shown
1	<H1>**18pt Heading**</H1>
2	<H2>**16pt Heading**</H2>
3	<H3>*14pt Heading*</H3>
4	<H4>**12pt Heading**</H4>
5	<H5>*11pt Heading*</H5>
6	<H6>10pt Heading</H6>

Figure 2.1: RFC 1866 recommended point sizes

Headings have a pre-defined space *before* and *after* the heading. Usually this is a 12-point line space.

You may think that these headings are not exactly gripping and you are not alone in that thought. We will offer some variation later in Part 2 when we discuss *style sheets*.

The `<center>` ... `</center>` tag

Headings are always left justified but you can centre a heading by enclosing it within the non-empty `<center>` tags. Do note the American spelling of the tag name! This tag can contain almost any other XHTML tag so that paragraphs, headings, images, etc., can be centred on a web page.

The `<blockquote>` ... `</blockquote>` tag

The `blockquote` tag not only creates a line space before and after its contained text, like the paragraph tag, but left indents the text to boot!

The empty `<hr/>` tag

This tag creates a horizontal rule (a line) across the entire screen. It is an empty tag because it does not contain any text which has to be formatted. It simply tells the browser to draw a line. It automatically puts a space before and after the actual rule. In other words, like the paragraph tag, it has some basic structure built into it.

For those of you familiar with HTML, you may be wondering what the forward slash is doing after the identifier - `hr`. In XHTML all tags must be closed. There are no exceptions. But empty tags do not have a corresponding ending tag. The way XHTML indicates that an empty tag is closed is by putting a forward slash *after* the identifier, whereas a non-empty closing tag has the forward slash *before* the identifier.

Be sure you appreciate this. `<h1>` ... `</h1>` is the correct way when using non-empty tags. `<hr/>` is the correct way when using an empty tag. However, to ensure backward compatibility with non-XHTML browsers, it is recommended that a space should be placed before the

15

forward slash. We shall use this syntax when using empty tags: `<hr />` and `<br />`.

The empty `<br />` tag

The break tag `<br />` is used to force the text which follows it to appear on the next line. It is an empty tag since it does not contain any text which has to be formatted. It simply tells the browser to place the following text onto the next line. Why not simply press the Enter key in our source code to force a carriage return just as we do in our word processor? Simply because carriage returns are regarded as *white space* and as such are ignored by the browser.

These two empty elements will work only in visual media and will produce no effect in other media such as aural.

White Space

In a document created with a word processor, we make use of the Enter key to force text onto a new line; we use tab keys and perhaps put extra spaces between words. All these techniques create *white space*. But the browser will remove all of them. If your source code has three spaces between one word and the next, the browser will convert them into a single *inter-word space*. Tabs are ignored. So how do we structure our Web documents?

Some tags *have* got built-in structure associated with their use. For example, the `<hr />` tag automatically puts a blank line before and after the line; the `<h1>` to `<h6>` heading tags ensure that the heading text automatically begins on a new line with a blank line before and after. The `<p>` tag will also automatically place its contained text with a line space before and after.

But some tags do not have any built-in structure and, consequently, we have to make use of other tags to enforce structure. If you want some text to start on a new line, when typing an address for example, then you must put in a tag to say so. This can be done by inserting the `<br />` - break tag. Let us combine all these tags to create the web page shown at the beginning of this Chapter.

```xml
<?xml version="1.0" encoding="UTF-8"?>
<!DOCTYPE html
    PUBLIC "-//W3C//DTD XHTML 1.0
    Transitional//EN"
"http://www.w3.org/TR/xhtml1/DTD/
    xhtml1-transitional.dtd">
<html xmlns="http://www.w3.org/1999/xhtml"
      xml:lang="en" lang="en">
<head>
<title>Basic Tags in XHTML</title>
</head>

<body>
<center>
<h3>An Author's Aside</h3>
</center>
<p>Betjeman, Sir John <br />
British poet known for his nostalgia for the
near past, his exact sense of place, and his
precise rendering of social nuance, which
made him widely read in England at a time
when much of what he wrote about was rapidly
vanishing.
</p>
<center>
<blockquote>
"I made hay whilst the sun shone, my work
sold. <br />
Now if the harvest is over and the world
cold, <br />
Give me the bonus of laughter, as I lose
hold."
</blockquote>
</center>
<hr />
<i>"The Last Laugh" by John Betjeman, 1974
<br />
b. Aug. 28, 1906, London, Eng. <br />
d. May 19, 1984, Trebetherick, Cornwall</i>
<hr />
</body> </html>
```

Exercise 2:

Type the above in your text editor and save the file as a text only file in a folder for your XHTML exercises. Add the `.htm` extension. Then open the file in your browser, for example Netscape or Internet Explorer. You should see something similar to the example given at the beginning of this Chapter.

Although this is an XHTML document, browsers which are not XHTML compliant will display it as though it had been written as pure HTML. Browsers are normally designed to ignore any tags which they cannot recognise. Consequently, the XHTML declaration will be ignored leaving the rest of the document looking like a pure HTML document.

One of the main considerations when developing this new language was that it should be backward compatible with existing HTML browsers. Thus, XHTML compatible browsers will still recognise pure HTML documents, and pure HTML browsers will ignore those parts of an XHTML document and just see it as a simple HTML document.

No more sloppy code

Because of the strict syntax imposed by XHTML, you will no longer get away with sloppy code. For example, what would an HTML browser do with the following incorrect code:

```
<h2>A Second Level Heading </h4>
```

Browser programs on our desk top computers have become bloated with the extra code required to 'interpret' the above in some meaningful way. Will the heading be level 2 or level 4? The new Internet access devices, such as palm tops and talking car phones, require more compact browser programs since they do not have the same memory capacity as our PCs. They will expect our XHTML code to conform to strict rules or else they will simply not display our pages.

Elements or Tags?

We have used the terms *tag* and *element* as though they were the same thing. It is time to be a little more exact.

Elements & Tags

Consider this source code example:

```
<h3>A Level 3 Heading </h3>
```

The entire code is formally called an *element*.

This element consists of:

an *opening* or *start* tag:	`<h3>`
a *closing* or *end* tag:	`</h3>`
a tag *identifier:*	h3

The text between the opening and closing tags is called the *content* or sometimes the *contained text* and will be formatted and displayed by the browser according to the tag specified by the author.

Converting to XHTML

Requirement	Example
all tag names must be in *lowercase*	`<p>` not `<P>`
all tags must be *closed* (terminated), even empty tags	`<p> ... </p>` `<hr />`
all XHTML documents must include <html>, <head> and <body> tags	See page 17
furthermore, the first element in the head must be a <title> element	`<title> some title </title>`

There are other requirements which we shall examine in the next chapter. But we have covered enough for now.

What you have learnt

We looked at some of the common elements in XHTML, noting that some are non-empty or container tags, whilst others are empty tags.

Empty tags must be closed by adding a forward slash *after* the tag identifier. We recommended that a space be placed before the forward slash. Although this is not an XHTML requirement, it will help HTML browsers to correctly identify such tags. Then both HTML and XHTML browsers will understand their meaning.

We discussed *white space* and how it is treated by browsers. Finally, we explained the difference between the terms elements and tags.

Test

1. Create a basic template which you can use for all your XHTML documents.

2. Is this correct XHTML?

```
<p>Here is a paragraph with this word in
<B>bold</B> and this following text back to
normal. </p>
```

3. Will your new XHTML files be displayed properly by those browsers which are only HTML compatible?

4. What tag would you use to create a horizontal line across the whole width of the screen? Does this tag also have automatic spacing before and after the line?

5. *"The* `<title>` *tag puts a title on to your Web page."* True or false?

6. If you accidentally put in two sets of `<body>` tags into your Web page, what would a browser do?

7. Which of the following tags are *empty* and which are *non-empty* tags:
`<head> <br/> <b> <title> <hr/> <h4>` ?

8. What is wrong with the following?

```
<head>The ABC plc Home Page</HEAD>
```

9. Why do we need to include a space after the tag identifier and the forward slash in empty tags: `<br />`?

10. Suppose you have saved an XHTML file as text only, but have forgotten to change the file extension to `.htm`, saving it as `fred.txt`, for example. What will the browser display if you open the `fred.txt` file?

3: The Block Elements

When we come to using style sheets in Part 2, it is sometimes necessary to distinguish between the types of elements. Consequently, we shall introduce the tags by type in the next few chapters. In this Chapter, we shall introduce the *block* elements. There are four broad types of elements:

- the block elements
- the inline descriptive elements
- the inline style elements
- a few miscellaneous elements

The Block Elements

```
<p>...</p>
<div>...</div>
<h1>...<h6>
<blockquote>...</blockquote>
```

These are elements which create an area or block for their contained text. We have already seen the `<p>..</p>` element which creates a normal paragraph of text. It has a line space before and after the text. It is a self contained block which is usually defined by a left and right margin, as well as a top and bottom line space. If another `<p>` element follows, that second block will have its own space:

> One paragraph of text contained within its own space.
>
> Another paragraph of text which again has its own space or block or area on the page.

Here are some more block elements:

`<div> ... </div>`
The division tag. This is similar to the `<p>` tag except that it does not leave a blank line before and after the contained text. It was not used much in HTML but has an important part to play in style sheets as we shall see later in Part 2.

`<h1> ... </h1> to <h6> ... </h6>`
These are the heading tags. There are six, each one provides a space before and after the heading text as well as displaying the text in different point sizes. See page 14.

`<blockquote> ... </blockquote>`
The `blockquote` tag not only creates a line space before and after its contained text but left indents the text to boot!

In the following we shall use all the above tags.

A Second Level Heading

Here is a paragraph of text using the paragraph tag. Note how there will be a line space after this paragraph.

This is a division - 1. The space before this text was created via the paragraph tag.
Here is another division - 2 - and this tag forces its content onto a new line with no line space.

> This is the content of the blockquote tag.
> Note how it is indented left and has a
> line space before and after the block of
> text.

Here is a line of text with no tag.

Here is the XHTML source code:

```
<?xml version="1.0" encoding="UTF-8"?>
<!DOCTYPE html
        PUBLIC "-//W3C//DTD XHTML 1.0
                Transitional//EN"
"http://www.w3.org/TR/xhtml1/DTD/xhtml1-
transitional.dtd">
<html xmlns="http://www.w3.org/1999/xhtml"
        xml:lang="en" lang="en">
<head>
<title>Third XHTML exercise</title>
</head>
<body>
<h2>
<center>A Second Level Heading </center>
</h2>
<p> Here is a paragraph of text using the
paragraph tag. Note how there will be a line
space after this paragraph. </p>
<div>This is a division - 1. The space before
this text was created via the paragraph
tag.</div>
<div>Here is another division - 2 - and this
tag forces its content onto a new line with
no line space. </div>
<blockquote>This is the content of the
blockquote tag. Note how it is indented left
and has a line space before and after the
block of text.</blockquote>
Here is a line of text with no tag.
</body>
</html>
```

Notes:
There is little to explain in the above code. The contents of each of the block elements are displayed according the structure mentioned above. We have the required declaration before the <html> element and have used one heading tag, one paragraph tag, two division tags, one

blockquote tag and some text which is not within any element.

However, there is one small detail which does need to be discussed. Note that the `<center>` element has been used. It is enclosed within the `<h2>` element. That is the correct way in XHTML.

```
<h2>
<center>A Second Level Heading </center>
</h2>                            CORRECT XHTML
```

Note how the `<center>` tags are enclosed (*nested* is the official term) within the outer `<h2>` tags. Likewise, we could have written:

```
<center>
<h2>A Second Level Heading </h2>
</center>                        CORRECT XHTML
```

where the `<h2>` tags are nested correctly within the outer `<center>` tags. Why all the fuss?

This is what you can do in HTML, but it is wrong, even according to the strict rules of HTML:

```
<h2><center>A Second Level Heading
</h2></center>                   WRONG
```

Many HTML authors do this and most HTML browsers would tolerate this despite the fact that it is illegal.

Here is another incorrect example which HTML browsers have been taught to tolerate, but which will not be tolerated by future XHTML browsers:

```
<p>
This is some text <b> in bold <i> and in
bold/italic </b> </i>
</p>                             WRONG
```

```
<p>
This is some text <b> in bold <i> and in
bold/italic </i> </b>
</p>                                    CORRECT XHTML
```

See how the `<i>` element is nested within the outer `<b>`
element. The corrected version is nested properly.
Although incorrect nesting is illegal in HTML, most browsers
were 'taught' to be tolerant of bad HTML code.

That is one simple example, but what about this?

```
<h2>A Second Level Heading</h4>
```

The heading levels are different and it is clearly wrong, an
example of sloppy HTML, but tolerated by most browsers.
What is so bad about that? It makes for much larger
browser programs! Also, one browser may interpret the
mistake in a different way to another. So, people viewing
such a web page may well see different things.

We need Discipline

Although the above examples are illegal, even in HTML,
many browsers have been taught to overlook such errors.
This has encouraged some web authors to write sloppy
code, develop bad habits, and so on. However, you will not
be allowed to get away with it in XHTML.

In order for sloppy code to be corrected, browser programs
became much larger than they needed to. That is no major
problem for PCs with their large memories and fast
processing power. But it will be a problem for the smaller
Internet access devices which are set to swamp the world.
Their XHTML browsers will have to be slender, much
smaller and compact than those on PCs.

One way of making browsers smaller is to reduce the
amount of checking they have to perform on source code. A
simple way of achieving this is to enforce a strict syntax.
That is why XHTML insists on:

- lowercase for all tag names
- that all tags must be closed, even the empty ones
- that all tags must be correctly nested

As we discuss in Chapter 21, XHTML is based on XML. XML has defined the syntax for XHTML and it is more strict than HTML in order to accommodate all the new devices. A correct XHTML document is one which adheres to the above rules. When it does, it is said to be *well formed*. That means, it is formed according to the rules of XML syntax.

The code will have to be correct (*well formed*) or it will not be recognised by the smaller devices, actually called *user agents* by the W3C. The smaller user agents will simply not display incorrectly written code.

How to Check your XHTML code

How can you check whether you have written a well formed XHTML document? It is difficult at present because we are in an interim period. XML, XHTML and CSS have all been specified by the W3C for several years now. The new devices are about to hit the market, some already have. But it will be a few years before they become commonplace. IE5 already accepts XML and therefore XHTML documents, but Netscape is not quite there. We are in between what has been and what has yet to become the norm.

Consequently, when you submit an XHTML document to IE5, it may not be a valid, correct, piece of source code, but it will work because it will be treated as an HTML document and any errors will be tolerated.

One of the truly useful programs I have come across whilst developing my experience of CSS and XHTML is the W3C validating service for both of the above. You can submit an XHTML document and/or a CSS style sheet over the Internet directly from your desk top's hard disc and you will be told whether it is correct or not. If not, the errors are pointed out.

The service is really fast. I have explained how to use the service in Chapter 20. You may wish to begin *validating* (as the process is called) your XHTML documents now.

Collapsing White Space

White space was discussed in the previous chapter. But there are two types of white space, one provides for *horizontal* spacing, such as the left indenting of a blockquote's content, and the *vertical* spacing between various blocks. How will a browser handle two consecutive block elements each of which has vertical space?

Collapsing White Space

Horizontal white space, such as tabs, extra spaces, and carriage returns, are 'collapsed' into a single inter-word space. Thus, twelve spaces between two words would result in a single space.

Vertical white space, lines before and after a tag (as with `<h1>`, `<p>`, `<blockquote>`, etc.) are also 'collapsed' into a single vertical space. In other words, when a `<p>` tag follows a previous `<p>` tag, there is only one line of white space, not two.

What you have learnt

With all the new Internet devices coming on to the market, such as TV web sets, palm top computers, speaking car devices, they will not have the same capacity as our desk top computers. The browser programs are going to have to be smaller and that means that they cannot make allowances for sloppy code.

We have seen that an XHTML document follows the rules of XML since the latter defined exactly how an XHTML document should be written. *(If this worries you, and I found it all very confusing at the beginning, do not worry just yet. It is explained in Chapter 21.)*

Consequently, all tags must be correctly *nested*, but the jargon term used is *well-formed*.

We have also looked at those elements which have a *block flow*, that is their contained text or content is placed within a given block with right-left and top-bottom margins.

We can now add the following to our list of do's and dont's when converting to XHTML:

Converting to XHTML

Requirement	Example
all tags must be well-formed - correctly nested	`<b>bold <i>and italic </i> text.</b>`

Test

1. What is the difference between the `<p>` element and the `<blockquote>` element?

2. How many rules of XHTML syntax does the following break?

```
<P>A paragraph of <b> bold text and <i> italic
</b> </i> text.
<div>Here is a division tag.<div>
```

3. What would happen if you ran the above code in a current browser?

4. How can you test whether you have written correct XHTML or not?

5. If a heading tag has an automatic line space after it and a paragraph tag has an automatic line space before, why would the following give only one line space between the two blocks and not two?

```
<h1>A Level 1 Heading </h1>
<p> A paragraph of text ... </p>
```

4: Inline Descriptive & Style Elements

In this Chapter, we shall look at those elements which have descriptive and stylistic meanings. First, what do we mean by *inline*? These elements are not *block* elements so they have no defined area as such. They are inline within some other block element. Here is an example of the inline `<cite>` tag which as you can see lies within a paragraph block element. It is used for citations:

```
<p>
"Beware the ides of March" is found in
<cite>Julius Caesar, Act 1, Scene 2</cite>. It
refers to: <i>15th March</i> and is uttered by
the Soothsayer.
</p>
```

The `<cite>` tag stands for a citation and most browsers will render its content in italics, thus:

"Beware the ides of March" is found in *Julius Caesar, Act 1, Scene 2*. It refers to: *15th March* and is uttered by the Soothsayer.

It has both a descriptive meaning (i.e. the tag tells you it is a citation) and a stylistic meaning because most browsers will display the contained text in italics.

On the other hand, the `<i>` tag is purely *stylistic*.

Some tags are purely descriptive and have no associated stylistic meaning, for example, the `<q>` element which stands for a *quotation*. It will not be displayed in any way different from normal text. So why bother with it? That depends entirely on what device will read your web pages. If your pages are always for display on a desk top computer, then you can forget many of the tags shown in Table 4.1, such as the `<q>` tag. It will make no difference whether it is there or not. However, should your web pages be destined, perhaps in the future, for several different devices, such as a desk top for the blind, a palm top or a speaking car phone, then these various tags will have more relevance. It is possible that the content of a quotation tag will be spoken in a different way so that the listener knows it is a quotation. Likewise, an abbreviation, such as ASCII if placed within the descriptive inline `<acronym>` element may be spelt out by letters but the tag ignored by visual browsers.

We need to remember that HTML was designed for the visual display of information on a desk top. The world is moving on and other devices are going to become more popular. It is expected that by the year 2005 (some think even 2002), 70% of Internet access will be by these other devices. So we are really thinking and planning for the future. That is one reason for moving towards XHTML. HTML was not designed to cope with these new devices.

Many of the elements in Table 4.1 were hardly ever used in HTML, but they may well take on more significance in the future. So you should be aware of their existence at the outset.

What now follows is a list of these descriptive and stylistic inline elements. After the Table, we show how some of the elements are displayed in both IE and Netscape. You are left to experiment with those which we do not show, if you so choose.

Inline Descriptive Elements	Comment
`<abbr> ... </abbr>`	Abbreviation. Purely descriptive. Has no stylistic meaning for most browsers.

Inline Descriptive Elements	Comment
`<acronym> ... </acronym>`	Acronym. Purely descriptive. Has no stylistic meaning for most browsers.
`<address> ... </address>`	Address. Descriptive - used for addresses. Usually displayed in italics.
`<cite> ... </cite>`	Citation. Usually displayed in italics.
`<code> ... </code>`	Code, such as source code. Usually displayed in a `monospaced` font.
`<dfn> ... </dfn>`	Definition. Usually displayed in italics.
`<em> ... </em>`	Emphasis. Usually displayed in italics.
`<q> ... </q>`	Quotation. Purely descriptive and has no stylistic display.
`<samp> ... </samp>`	Sample for literal characters. Usually displayed in italics.
`<span> ... </span>`	Span for defining a span of text. It is used in conjunction with style sheets.
`<strong> ... </strong>`	Strong. Displays text in bold.
`<var> ... </var>`	Variable. Used to describe its content as a variable name, e.g. in programming source code. Usually displayed in italics.

Table: 4.1

The following are purely inline stylistic elements.

Inline Stylistic Elements	Comment
`<big> ... </big>`	Content displayed in a larger font.
`<b> ... </b>`	Content displayed in **bold**.
`<i> ... </i>`	Content displayed in *italic*.

Inline Stylistic Elements	Comment
`<kbd> ... </kbd>`	Keyboard. Content displayed in `monospaced` font.
`<u> ... </u>`	Underline. Content displayed in <u>underline</u>.
`<small> ... </small>`	Content displayed in a smaller font.
`<strike> ... </strike>`	Content displayed in ~~strikethrough~~.
`<sub> ... </sub>`	Content displayed in subscript. H_2O
`<sup> ... </sup>`	Content displayed in superscript. 20^0C.
`<tt> ... </tt>`	Teletype. Content displayed in `monospaced` font.

Table 4.2

We use various inline style tags in the following source code. You may wish to experiment with some of the others.

```
<body>
<hr />
<h3>Some In line styles </h3>
<hr />
<div>Text in <abbr>Abbreviation tag</abbr> -
     Descriptive only </div>
<div>Text in <em>Emphasis tag</em>
    - Descriptive and stylistic</div>
<div>Text in <q>Quotation tag</q>
    - Descriptive only </div>
<div>Text in <samp>Sample tag</samp>
    - Descriptive and stylistic </div>
<div>Text in <var>Variable tag</var>
    - Descriptive and stylistic </div>
<div>Text in <big>Big tag</big>
    - Stylistic only</div>
<div>Text in <small>Small tag</small>
    - Stylistic only </div>
<div>Text in <strike>Strikethrough tag</strike>
    - Stylistic only </div>
<div>Text in <sup>Superscript tag</sup>
    - Stylistic only </div> </body>
```

34

Some In line styles

Text in Abbreviation tag - Descriptive only
Text in *Emphasis tag* - Descriptive and stylistic
Text in Quotation tag - Descriptive only
Text in `Sample tag` - Descriptive and stylistic
Text in *Variable tag* - Descriptive and stylistic
Text in Big tag - Stylistic only
Text in Small tag - Stylistic only
Text in ~~Strikethrough tag~~ - Stylistic only
Text in ^Superscript tag^ - Stylistic only

For my taste, there is too large a gap between the horizontal rules and the heading text. It has been correctly collapsed as mentioned on page 29. When we come to using style sheets, we shall see how we can rectify this.

The <address>...</address> element

The address element has undergone a change. Originally, it was simply used to format text in italics, perhaps at a point size lower than normal text and it was used as an inline element. Today, browsers have now made it a block element. It behaves like the division element, in that it puts its contained text on a new line and any text that follows the closing address tag will be placed on the next line, but it will also italicise its content.

Its main purpose is to create what is called a signature or authorship information. By convention, all web pages should have the author's or organisation's name, the date the document was written or last amended and an e-mail address. In this sense, the address tag is an example of a block element as well as being descriptive (authorship information) and stylistic (italics). However, as with the <blockquote> element, a break tag is required to force text on to the next line.

Quotation

> Here's a fish hangs in the net like a poor man's right in the law.
> 'Twill hardly come out.

Author: William Shakespeare
Died: Saturday, 23rd April, 1616
e-mail: w.shakespeare@globe.com

```
<body>
<h2>Quotation</h2>
<blockquote> Here's a fish hangs in the net
like a poor man's right in the law. <br />
'Twill hardly come out.</blockquote>
<address>
Author: William Shakespeare <br />
Died: Saturday, 23rd April, 1616 <br />
e-mail: w.shakespeare@globe.com
</address>
</body>
</html>
```

Why Block & Inline Elements were invented

Originally, HTML was designed purely to display text in a simple manner. The appearance of the text was of little concern to those who began using the language, mainly researchers and academics. Their main consideration was to pass text between one another where the emphasis was on structure, not on colour, font types, size, etc., all the things we normally associate with current word processors.

It was much later that Web authors became interested in the appearance of their web pages.

Consequently, the original HTML used certain tags to force structure into a web page, such as the `<p>` and `<h1>` tags. These are our block elements and they have built-in structure. To emphasise certain words, *inline* tags were used such as the `<b>` and the `<i>` elements.

What you have learnt

We have seen that elements are divided into *block* and *inline* elements. The block elements create their own space. Inline elements have no space of their own. They can be either purely *descriptive*, such as `<q>`, or purely *stylistic* such as `<i>`. Some descriptive elements may be stylistic as well, such as `<cite>`.

5: Lists

We shall see how to create lists in this chapter. Should you already be familiar with these features, just make sure you know the correct way to write these elements in XHTML by glancing at the source code of the examples.

Lists

We all need to create lists from time to time. There are three main elements used in XHTML to provide such lists:

- the unordered list - `<ul>` ... `</ul>`
- the ordered list   - `<ol>` ... `</ol>`
- the definition list - `<dl>` ... `</dl>`

Note that they are all examples of block elements. They have there own space on a web page.

Unordered List - `<ul>` ... `</ul>`

This is the unordered list consisting of a series of short lines, each marked with the `<li>` element. Each line is usually marked by a round bullet or similar symbol and the text is indented from the symbol. If text wraps to the next line, it is aligned with the indent. It is called unordered to contrast it with the ordered `<ol>` tag which creates a numbered list (ordered as 1, 2, 3 etc.). Suppose I want the following:

UL

Here is an unordered list, note the bullets:

- List item 1
- List item 2. Let's see what happens when this list item flows over to another line.
- List item 3

39

```
<body>
<h1>UL </h1>
Here is an unordered list, note the bullets:
<ul>
  <li>List item 1 </li>
  <li>List item 2. Let's see what happens when
this list item flows over to another line. </li>
  <li>List item 3</li>
</ul>
</body>
```

Note that the `<li>` tag requires a closing `</li>` tag.
HTML does not demand the closing tag, but XHTML does!

Ordered List - `<ol>` ... `</ol>`

This is similar to `<ul>` except that list items are numbered.
In the following example, note how `<ol>` may be nested to
produce a second level of indentation. (The `<ul>` can also
have other levels of indentation.) Each list item in the
second level is, again, marked with the `<li>` element and
must contain its own non-empty pair of `<ol>` tags.

```
<body>
<h3>OL </h3>
Here is an ordered list, note the numbering:
<ol>
  <li>List item 1</li>
  <li>List item 2. Let's see what happens when
      this list item flows over to another line.
  </li>
      <ol>
          <li>substep 1</li>
          <li>substep 2</li>
      </ol>
  <li>List item 3</li>
</ol>
</body>
```

OL

Here is an ordered list, note the numbering:

1. List item 1
2. List item 2. Let's see what happens when this list item flows over to another line.
    1. substep 1
    2. substep 2
3. List item 3

Notes:

1. The use of indents helps to make the XHTML source document easier to read.

2. With the `<ul>` list, most browsers show a different bullet style for the lower levels of indentation. Again, what will be produced depends on which browser is being used.

3. You can specify the type of bullet and the numbering style to be used. This is done by adding an *attribute* to the `<ul>` and `<ol>` tags. See page 48 in the next Chapter where we discuss attributes in detail.

The Definition List - `<dl>` ... `</dl>`

The definition list is used to create hanging lists. It does *not* take the `<li>` element, but two other tags, `<dt>` ... `</dt>` and `<dd>` .. `</dd>`. It is intended for a list of named items, such as a *Glossary of Terms*, (the definition term - `<dt>`) and an accompanying paragraph of definition or explanation (the `<dd>`).

The entire list of items must be enclosed within the `<dl>` ... `</dl>` pair. The contents of a `<dl>` is a sequence of `<dt>` and `<dd>` pairs. The browser automatically indents the text of the `<dd>` element.

Here is an example, note the required closing tags:

```
<head>
<title> Exercise for the DL, DTs and DDs
</title>
</head>
<body>
<h2>Glossary</h2>
<dl>
 <dt>The DL tag </dt>
  <dd>Stands for a Definition List</dd>
 <dt>The DT tag </dt>
  <dd> The term which is to be defined - usually
a short phrase. </dd>
 <dt>The DD tag </dt>
  <dd> The actual definition of the term in the
DT tag. Lengthy definitions extending over
several lines will align correctly. </dd>
</dl>
</body>
```

Glossary

The DL tag
    Stands for a Definition List
The DT tag
    The term which is to be defined - usually a short phrase.
The DD tag
    The actual definition of the term in the DT tag. Lengthy
    definitions extending over several lines will align correctly.

Lists with Different Media Types

Lists can be useful when your page is to be displayed on different media types. They transfer well to both voice and Braille media browsers and should be used in preference to tables (see Chapter 17).

There are two more bulleted list tags, seldom used, but we need to know what they do in case we meet them in someone else's source code. They are the <dir> and <menu> tags and both behave identically to the <ul> tag. Instead of <ul> we use <menu> or <dir>. In the following,

we show the <menu> tag, but try it out with <dir> as well
by substituting menu for dir.

<dir> ... </dir> & <menu> ... </menu>

These are similar to the <ul>, where each list item is
bulleted. Most browsers make no distinction between
<menu> <dir> and <ul>.

Here is an example of the <menu> tag:

```
<head><title> Menu Example</title></head>
<body>
<h3>MENU</h3>
<menu>
   <li>List item 1</li>
   <li>List item 2. Let's see what happens when
this list item flows over to another line. </li>
   <li>List item 3</li>
</menu>
</body>
```

There are two more elements we shall discuss in this
chapter. The first is the <pre> ... </pre> tag and the
second is how to insert comments within our code.

Preformatted - <pre>

This is suitable for text which needs to be displayed in a
monospaced font. Unlike other tags, the <pre> element
preserves line breaks and extra spaces. It was originally
intended as a method for creating simple columns.

```
<body>
<h2>Use of PRE tag </h2>
What   follows   is   some   text   which   has   been
formatted in a monospaced font using PRE.
<pre>
Column A        Column B
  Fred            Mary
  £34.56          £45.69
</pre>
</body>
```

Use of PRE tag

What follows is some text which has been formatted in a monospaced font using PRE.

```
Column A          Column B
   Fred             Mary
  £34.56           £45.69
```

Text within the `<pre>` tags is rendered (displayed) in a fixed-width typewriter font, usually Courier. The `<pre>` element cannot contain the `img`, `object`, `big`, `small`, `sub`, or `sup` elements. (We have not yet discussed some of these elements. They are mentioned here for your future reference.)

It is rare today to see web pages using the `<pre>` tag. It was employed in earlier days for browsers which could not display columns via the `<table>` tag, see Chapter 17.

Adding Comments

Comments may be added to an XHTML document for whatever purpose the author wishes, typically to explain to others who may have to maintain the web page what the author was trying to attempt, perhaps warnings about changes in staff or the start date of a new pricing system. The comments are not displayed by the browser, unless someone views the source code.

Comments begin with `<!--` and end with `-->` There must be no space between the exclamation mark '!' and the `--`. All other spaces are treated as part of the comment.

The ABC plc Home Page

- List of Staff Members
- Our Products
- Customer Support

The entire comment is ignored by the browser and is seen *only* in the source document.

```
<head><title>Comments Example </title></head>
<body >
<h3>The ABC plc Home Page</h3>
<ul>
<li>List of Staff Members </li>
<!-- The current MD is leaving in Sept. 2001.
Update list with name of new MD. -->
<li>Our Products</li>
<!--    Price  changes  take  place  every  Sept.
Update the price list. -->
<li>Customer Support</li>
</ul>
</body>
```

What you have learnt

We have seen how to create lists and mentioned that they transfer well to other media browsers such as Braille and voice. They are all examples of block elements.

The <pre> tag and the use of comments were also introduced.

So far our web pages have not been particularly interesting. They will appear typically in Times Roman with black text on a white background. Interesting effects are achieved through the use of *attributes* and style sheets. We shall discuss attributes in the next section. It is through attributes that we can create hypertext and put images into our pages.

6: Attributes & Hypertext links

What are attributes? They further define the use of the tag itself and must be placed in the starting tag. The attribute is separated from the tag ID by a space (not a comma). They usually take the form of: <ID *attributename* = "*somevalue*">

For example, in the previous Chapter we looked at the ordered list using the <ol> element. When displayed by a browser, the list items were numbered - 1 2 3, etc. But supposing we wanted Roman numerals or letters. Then we would use an *attribute*. Using the example from the previous chapter, let us

ol with panache
i. List item 1
ii. List item 2.
a. substep 1
b. substep 2
iii. List item 3

decide to use small Roman numerals for the outer items, and lowercase letters for the inner items.

Here is the code which does it:

```
<ol type="i">
  <li>List item 1  </li>
  <li>List item 2. </li>
      <ol type="a">
          <li>substep 1</li>
          <li>substep 2</li>
      </ol>
  <li>List item 3</li>
</ol>
```

Notes:
1. The only change is the inclusion of an attribute in both the opening <ol> tags: type="i" and type="a"

```
type    is the attribute
=       separates the attribute from its value
"i"     is the value, here asking for small Roman numerals
"I"     large Roman numerals
"a"     small letters or "A" large letters
```

disc|square|circle   will set the bullet style for the `<ul>` or `<li>` tag:

```
<li type="disc"> <ul type="circle">
```

2. In XHTML *all* attributes *must* take a value. (This was not always the case in HTML.) The equals sign simply separates the attribute from its value. All values *must* be enclosed in double quotes. Again, this was not a strict requirement for HTML, but is rigorously enforced in XHTML.

3. The attributes are always placed in the opening tag with a space (never a comma) separating the tag ID from the attribute. Sometimes we need to include more than one attribute, in which case a single space separates one attribute from another:

```
<tagID attribute1 = "value" attribute2="VALUE">
```

4. In the above, there is a space before and after the equals for one of the attributes and not for the other. Both forms are valid, so the choice is yours.

5. Attributes, like tag identifiers, must be in lowercase. However, the values may be in any case, as shown in the above example.

Types of Attributes

We could go into a long discussion here about the various terms used to describe different types of attributes. For our purpose we can divide them into two categories. The first is the *presentational* attributes such as the one given above which allows you to choose the style of enumeration for an ordered list. Here is another presentational attribute which selects a background colour for the entire web page via the `bgcolor` attribute. It is placed in the opening tag of the `<body>` element: `<body bgcolor="yellow">`

We need not bother with many of these presentational attributes because we can do far better with style sheets because they have more style options. In any case, many of the presentational attributes used in classic HTML are deprecated[1] in favour of style sheets.

The other type of attributes are those which we *must* use in order to create hypertext links and images. These are the ones we shall be looking at in this section and the next, and, to give them a name of some sort, we shall call them the *required* or *essential* attributes. *(But that is just my term for those attributes which we do need to know about.)*

The presentational attributes are for use with those browsers which do not recognise style sheets and here there is a problem for Web authors. At what stage do we begin to assume that all our readers have browsers which can recognise style sheets so that we no longer need to use presentational attributes? At some stage, we just have to assume (and pray!) that our readers will have at least version 4 of Netscape and IE version 5. *(That is the assumption I now make when creating web pages.)*

Content versus Presentation

It is fundamental to XHTML that we appreciate the difference between *content* and its *presentation*. One of the good features of writing XHTML is that we can separate the content of a web page from its presentational formatting. That is why the first part of this text is mainly concerned with how to use XHTML in order to create the content for our web pages. In Part 2, we discuss how to make our documents look pretty. When we come to that stage, we

---

[1] *Deprecate* is a term used by W3C to mean that in future revisions of XHTML, the attribute will be phased out. Therefore, it is not wise to use deprecated attributes or tags.

shall see that it is possible for someone else to impose a style sheet on the contents of our web pages. For example, certain organisations enforce a common 'house style' that all pages must adhere to. Consequently, some web page authors are responsible solely for the content, via XHTML, and others for its presentation via CSS.

In pure HTML the `<font>` tag was the main means whereby content was given style. It was used to specify the colour, typeface and size for text. It is a *deprecated* tag, which simply means that it will be tolerated for the time being, but will be written out (killed off) at some future time. Many other tags in HTML could additionally take formatting attributes to enhance the appearance of text, images, tables and the entire web page itself. For example, the `bgcolor` attribute in the `<body>` element:

```
<body bgcolor = "yellow">
```

But many of these attributes, such as the `bgcolor` in the `body` tag, are deprecated. So, we shall have to stop using them at some stage. Style sheets offer so much more control over appearance, that it is a waste of your time if I mention all the presentational attributes.

For those who are really interested in knowing how web pages were made to look good in HTML, read my book, "How to create web pages using HTML", second edition, in this Babani series. It is possible that some of you may inherit pure HTML documents which you have to maintain or amend. In which case, you may need to be able to recognise such attributes. For the moment, we discuss only those attributes which are essential to XHTML, such as those required to create hypertext links and to insert images into our pages.

The Essential Attributes for the `<a>` element

For those of you who know how to create hypertext links, you can move on to another section. What follows is pure HTML but written in strict XHTML syntax.

The `<a>` ... `</a>` tag

To create hypertext in XHTML the **`<a>...</a>`** container tag is used. Whatever is typed (is contained) between these tags becomes *hypertext* and, typically, will be coloured blue and underlined by the browser. The `<a>` stands for *anchor*, but by itself it is useless, it requires attributes before it can do anything useful. One of its main attributes is `href` - meaning a *hypertext reference* which provides the address from where the document can be retrieved.

The `href` Attribute

When a hypertext link is clicked, the document referenced may be:

- held on another server *anywhere* in the world
- held in the *same directory* as the current document
- or, some other position within the *same document*

The last one is useful when a document is long and a user may wish to move immediately to a particular part of that document without having to use the scroll bar.

It is the value of the `href` attribute of the anchor tag which provides the necessary information for the Web browser to find and display the referenced text.

For example, if I wanted the phrase 'Section 3' to become a hypertext link, it would have to be enclosed within the pair of `<a>` tags. The browser will then automatically make it blue and underlined.

There is more information in **Section 3** for those who are interested.

Here is the relevant code:

```
There is more information in
<a   href="http://www.abc.co.uk/courses.htm">
Section 3
</a> for those who are interested.
```

51

If a reader clicks this phrase, the browser will look at the value of the `href` attribute to find the address of where the document is kept. The browser sends this address to its local web server. If the web server is connected to the Internet, it can request a copy of the document from the web server holding that document. Once it has been received, the local web server passes it on to the browser which can now display the page.

The value of the `href` attribute is a URL[2]. We shall discuss this now and then look at some examples.

When a Document is held at a Different Site

To point to documents held at a site other than your own local Web server, the link must contain a *complete* URL.

URL (Uniform Resource Locator)

A complete URL consists of:

- the *method* by which a document is accessed
- the unique address of the *site* (server) where the document is held
- the name of the document - *file name*

Example:

```
http://www.ic.ac.uk/courses.htm
```

`http` is the Web's own method for accessing and transferring documents between different Web servers. It stands for the *h*yper*t*ext *t*ransfer *p*rotocol. It is a set of rules (the *protocol*) used by network servers for transmitting data.

`://` is a separator marking off the transmission protocol from the rest of the URL

`www.ic.ac.uk` is the site address of where the document is stored, and refers to the Web server (*www*) at Imperial College (*ic*) which is part of the academic community (*ac*) in

---

[2] A URL and an expected new way of identifying resources called a URN - Uniform Resource Name are now both referred to as a URI - Uniform Resource Identifier. But it means the same as URL.

the United Kingdom (*uk*). Each site has its own unique Web site address, rather like each household has its own unique postal address or telephone number. Indeed, the site address *is* a set of four numbers each separated by a full stop. This is why you may sometimes see numbers rather than letters in some URLs: `http://123.45.06.78/`

Names are easier to type and to remember rather than numbers. The names used are converted to numbers by the Web server. It is rather like looking up a telephone number when you are given a name.

`courses.htm` is the actual file name of the Web page held in the server's storage discs.

Clicking on **Section 3** would cause the browser to look at the value of the `href` attribute, and request that document, using the *http* protocol, from the Web server which is holding that page. Once our browser has received a copy, it can then display the document onto our screen.

Thus, if someone at their office machine in, say, Houston, Texas, was reading a document containing:

Courses held at Imperial College, London
Courses held at Oxford University, England
Courses held at Birkbeck College, London

and they chose the courses at Imperial, the Web browser would contact the Web server at Imperial College, obtain a copy of `courses.htm` and display the document on the computer screen in Houston, Texas.

```
<a href=
    "http://www.ic.ac.uk/courses/courses.htm">
    Courses </a>
    held at Imperial College, London <br />
<a href=
    "http://www.ox.ac.uk/maindir/oxcourses.htm">
    Courses </a>
    held at Oxford University, England <br />
```

It should go without saying that the URL must be typed in correctly, just as we must correctly type *any* address or telephone number. This includes the correct name of the document. If the URL contains a mistake, the browser will not be able to retrieve the document. Case is significant in URLs.

You could, of course, simply display the URL as ordinary text and ask the reader to type it in their browser's address location box. But XHTML offers hypertext as an alternative. When a reader clicks the hypertext, the end result is the equivalent of the reader typing the address into the browser's location box.

Document at the Same Site

Should a document referenced by some hypertext reside in the same *directory* (folder) as the document currently on the screen, a shorter form of the URL can be used. Such links are called *partial* or *relative* addresses.

```
for more information
<a href="doc2.htm"> click here.</a>
```

for more information <u>click here.</u>

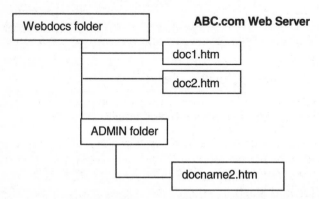

The above code will assume that the document pointed to (doc2.htm) by the href attribute is another file in the

54

same directory and on the *same* server as the actual document you are looking at.

Sometimes, people on my XHTML courses find this a little puzzling, so let us spell out what is happening.

Say the original document (`doc1.htm`) is currently displayed because the user:

- typed in the complete URL in a browser's location box
- used a search engine to find the document
- clicked a hypertext link in some other document

In all cases, the browser will have been given a complete URL, for example:

```
http://www.abc.com/webdocs/doc1.htm
```

It knows where it went in order to get the `doc1.htm` page. If this page refers to another document, say `doc2.htm`, which is in the *same* folder as the `doc1.htm` page, the web author of `doc1.htm` needs to provide only a partial address:

```
<a href="doc2.htm"> a second document </a>
```

Here is a second document which you may like to see.

When a second document is clicked, the browser looks at the `href`'s value and sees just the name of the document. It will fill in the missing bits because it knows where it found the original `doc1.htm`.

Thus: ***http://www.abc.com/webdocs/***`doc2.htm`

The browser assumes that this new document is lying side by side in the same folder as the original `doc1.htm`.

Should the document be in a sub-directory of the current folder in which the document you are reading is stored, then that sub-directory would have to be included. Do not put a forward slash in front of the sub-directory. Thus, if a document, say `doc2.htm`, **references** `docname2.htm` which is in a sub-directory named `admin`, then the following code would be used:

```
<a href="admin/docname2.htm"> ... </a>
```

Since the browser knows the address of where it found `doc2.htm`, it will complete the partial address as follows;

*http:/www.abc.com/webdocs/*admin/docname2.htm

These are called *relative* or *partial* addresses simply because the path specified to the other document is relative to the location (directory) of the current page being displayed by the browser.

Advantages of using Relative Links

One advantage of using relative links is that it reduces typing and the risk of mis-typing. But there is another and more important advantage. Let us suppose that one main document has links to several other documents. The main document and all the others are stored in the same folder on the Web server. Should it become necessary for the Web Manager to move all the documents to a different site or folder, all the relative links in the main document do not have to be updated. The relative links will become relative to the new location of the main document. Of course, the original URL of the main document will have to be changed so that users can reference its new location. But, once they have done so, all links in the main document become relative to its new location.

Moving within the Same Document

The example in Figure 6.1 is a single document which has information about the various courses a Centre may offer. The reader can immediately jump to the one he or she is interested in, or find details of how to get to the Centre, how to register, etc., by clicking on the relevant piece of hypertext (underlined in the example).

To create a link in a document to some other point within the *same* document, the `href` must contain a pointer to that position and make use of the `name` attribute at that point.

Clicking on the hypertext 'Venue' will cause the browser to search for the marker `venue` elsewhere in the same document and display what is at that point at the *top* of the window.

```
<a href="#venue">Venue</a> - How to Find Us
```

Training Centre Courses

Courses
Venue   - How to Find Us
How to Register
Course fees

Courses:

Excel for Windows
HTML
JavaScript
Mac Operating System
Unix Operating System
Windows 2000
Word for Windows
....

Venue
The Training Centre is situated in ..... etc. ...

Registration Details
To register for a course .... etc. ...

Course Fees
Fees for the courses vary .... etc. ...

Course Details
   Excel for Windows .... etc. ...

....

Figure 6.1

Note how the `href` attribute has no site address, no document name, just a hash (#) symbol followed by `venue` The name `venue` is invented by the author and its case is significant!!

The hash symbol tells the browser that it has to look in the *same* document and not go off over the Internet to find another document. However, there must clearly be some point in the document which effectively says: "I am the place called `venue`." This is achieved by marking that point with *another* `<a>` pair of tags which has a `name` attribute with the value `venue`.

```
<a name="venue"> Here I am, you found me.</a>
```

Likewise, a click on the *How to Register* hypertext would jump to an `<a>` tag with a `name` attribute with the value `H2Reg`. Note that the # symbol is required in the `href`'s value followed by the name of the place to go to; whereas the `name` attribute's value has only the *value*, no hash symbol.

```
<a href="#venue">Venue</a> - How to Find Us<br />
<a href="#H2Reg">How to Register</a> <br />
.....
.....
<h3><a name="venue">Venue</a></h3>
The Training Centre is situated in ..... etc.
... etc. ...
<h3><a NAME="H2Reg">Registration Details</a>
</h3>
To register for a course .... etc. ...
```

Browsers do not display the text contained within `<a>` tags with a `name` attribute in any special way. However, it is quite likely that the author may wish to format that text with, say, a level 3 heading. It is important that the pair of `<a>` tags are contained *within* the `<h3>` format tags. Thus, if 'Registration Details' were formatted as:

```
<h3>Registration Details</h3>
```

and we now wanted to convert it into a hyperlink, then the
`<h3>` tags should contain/enclose the pair of `<a>` tags thus:

```
<h3>   <a name="H2Reg">Registration Details </a>
</h3>                              CORRECT XHTML
```

NOT:

```
<a   name="H2Reg">
<h3>Registration Details </h3>
</a>                              WRONG
```

Finally, since the text contained within `<a>` tags with a
`name` attribute is not displayed in any special way, there is
actually no need for any text to be placed within the pair.
Thus, both the following are perfectly valid. It is the `name`
attribute which forces the browser to locate that point and
place it at the top of the browser window.

```
<h3><a name="come_here">Courses</a> </h3>
                          or
<a name="come_here"> </a> <h3> Courses</h3>
```

Hypertext & Courtesy

It is customary to enable users to return to the starting point
of a long document without forcing them to use the scroll
bar. Let us suppose that a user has clicked on a hypertext
reference which calls up another part of the same
document. Having read the information, the user may now
wish to return to the beginning of the document (typically a
list of contents, an index, etc.). The author should add a
hypertext link back to that point in the document.

Likewise, an author may have several web documents
referenced by one main document. It is useful to allow the
reader to be able to return to the main document once one
of the others has been digested. This is easily done by
putting in links in the other documents which return to the
main document. This little courtesy saves the user having to

click, perhaps several times, on the browser's *Go Back* button. Here is an example.

```
<head>
<title>'Document A' code - docA.htm </title>
</head>
<body>
<h2>Main Contents List</h2>
<ul>
   <li><a href="intr-org.htm">
      Introduction to our Organisation</a>
   </li>
   <li><a href="staff.htm">
        Staff Members</a> </li>
   <li><a href="pgcrs.htm"> </li>
        Post Graduate Courses</a>
   <li> .. etc .. </li>
</ul>
</body>
```

In Document A - called docA.htm:

Main Contents List

- Introduction to our Organisation
- Staff Members
- Post Graduate Courses

Clicking on *'Post Graduate Courses'* in Document A would display Document B. Clicking on *'Return to the Main Contents List'* in Document B would force the browser to locate and re-display Document A.

In Document B - called pgcrs.htm

Post Graduate Courses

Here is a list of our post-graduate courses.
- Chemical Research
- Concrete Structures
- Environmental Engineering
Return to the Main Contents List

60

```
<head>
<title> 'Document B' code - pgcrs.htm</title>
<!-- post graduate courses -->
</head>

<body>
<h2>Post Graduate Courses</h2>
Here is a list of our post-graduate courses.
....... etc ...
<a href="docA.htm">
    Return to the Main Contents List</a>
</body>
```

How to do it within a single document:

```
<h2><A name="Top">Contents List</a></h2>
      Venue
      Courses
      Fees
....... etc. .....
....... etc. .....
<a href="#Top">Return to Top</a>
```

Contents List

....
.... etc ... a really long document

....
Return to Top

Clicking on *'Return to Top'* would cause the browser to search for the marker `'Top'` attached as the value of a `name` attribute within the same document. In other words, it would cause the browser to re-display the same document with the Contents List positioned at the top of the screen.

Port Numbers

`:1080` Sometimes, you may see what is called a *port* number attached to the web site address and preceded by a colon (:)

`http://www.abc.com:1066/docname.htm`

61

Fortunately, this is not something we have to worry about. That burden is part of the joy of being a Web Master or Web Manager. It is sometimes convenient for Web Masters to arrange that certain web documents are stored in a special area on their Web server's discs. Usually, most web pages would be accessed via the standard/default port, which does not usually have to be given. But if one of the special documents is requested, then the URL must specify that the document can be found only by going through a particular port. These are simply numbers but must be specified if given in a URL. It will be the Web Master who decides whether our documents are to be put in a special folder and, therefore, would need a port number or not. Our only concern is when we publish the URL of our Web page to the public at large, in which case we would have to include the port number.

Other Protocols

`http` indicates the Web protocol, but many other protocols can be used as well.

`file:` Many authors create their web pages on their home or office PC. The `file` protocol causes the browser to load a file from the locally accessible disc system, i.e. the local hard disc.

`mailto:` E-mail protocol for sending messages from the browser. The e-mail address follows the colon (:).

`news:` This is the protocol for news/discussion/chat groups - the group name follows the colon.

`ftp:` file transport protocol. An earlier Internet tool used for transferring files. It is still possible to see URLs using this protocol.

`gopher:` the gopher protocol was used to search for information on the Web in the days before browsers. It was an early type of search engine.

`telnet:` an earlier Internet tool for accessing resources at another site. Essentially it allowed authorised outsiders to poke about in folders to see what was there.

Sending e-mails via mailto:

It is common for Web documents to include e-mail addresses which when clicked will call up the browser's e-mail program so that a reader can send a message to the author. It saves the reader from having to call up his/her own e-mail program and then having to return to the browser to carry on reading.

```
If you have any comments why not
<a href= "mailto:j.smith@abc.co.uk">
e-mail me? </a> I would be most grateful.
```

The above would look like:

If you have any comments why not <u>e-mail me?</u> I would be most grateful.

A browser's e-mail window has the typical: TO: FROM: SUBJECT: boxes and a bigger box for the message. The reader fills in the message and clicks on the SEND button all without leaving the Web page he/she is reading.

Note that both the `mailto:` and the `news:` have just one colon after the protocol, not the usual `://` as with the *http* protocol. This is simply because both systems existed long before the Web and browsers. Therefore, they knew nothing (nor cared) about the syntax of the *http* protocol.

```
Allergies <a href="news:alt.med.allergy">
try this.</a>
```

would produce:

Allergies <u>try this</u>.

What you have learnt

We have seen that *attributes* further extend the use of a tag. In some tags, such as the anchor tag , `<a>`, the `href` or the `name` attributes are required, otherwise the tag itself becomes useless.

All attributes must take a *value* and the attribute itself must be in lowercase.

The *value* must be either double quoted, the norm, or single quoted and, strange to relate, can be in any case.

We mentioned that presentational attributes are not used to any great extent in XHTML and we shall not cover them in any detail in this text, preferring instead to concentrate on style sheets.

Converting to XHTML

Requirement	Example

All attributes must take a value. The attribute name must be in lowercase and the value must be in single or double quotes.	`<body bgcolor="teal">`
	
	or
	
	`<body bgcolor='teal'>`

The value may be in any or even a mixed case. The latter is not advised.	or `<body bgcolor="TeAl">`

Test

1. How would you colour the background of your web page? You may wish to experiment with some of the colours given on the next page.

2. When the `bgcolor` attribute goes for good, how will you be able to give a background colour to your web pages?

3. Which attribute is used to reference a point within the same document?

4. How can you get your reader to send you an e-mail message without leaving the browser?

5. You want a hypertext link to some other document but you have forgotten the URL, what can you do about it?

Colour Names

There are sixteen common colour names which most browsers can recognise. Those marked with an asterisk are not always accepted by some browsers. It would be safer to use their hexadecimal values. See page 154 for how to find the hexadecimal values of any colour.

Colour name	Hex value	Colour name	Hex value
black	"#000000"	green	"#00FF00"
silver	"#C0C0C0"	lime	"#008000"
gray (US spelling)	"#808080"	olive	"#808000"
white	"#FFFFFF"	yellow	"#FFFF00"
maroon	"#800000"	navy	"#000080"
red	"#FF0000"	blue	"#0000FF"
purple	"#800080"	teal	"#008080"
fuchsia	"#FF00FF"	aqua	"#00FFFF"
* lightblue	"#CCFFFF"	* lightgreen	"#8DF78D"
* lightyellow	"#F1EF95"	* pink	"#FF99CC"

7: Putting Images into a Web Page

Adding an image or picture can brighten up your web pages. Indeed, it was only once the image element was added to a later version of HTML that the Web really began to be accepted. But, it should be remembered that each image is a separate file and it takes time for the browser to locate it over the Internet and then display it. The bigger the image, the longer it takes to retrieve and display.

If you already know how to insert images into your web pages, you can skip to the next Chapter where we summarise all the XHTML syntax, but be sure you check the correct syntax for the `image` *element and the* `border` *attribute.*

Most Web browsers can display images in GIF (`.gif`), JPEG (`.jpeg` or `.jpg`) and PNG (`.png`) formats. We have more to say about these formats later.

The `<img />` tag

An image can be:

- inserted by itself anywhere in a document - just for decorative purposes
- inserted along with text
- inserted as a hypertext link so that when clicked it will display another document or image

We shall now see how to accomplish the above.

Inserting an Image just for Decoration

The `<img />` tag is an empty element. However, it must contain at least one attribute, `src` (source), telling the browser where to find the image. When images for a web page are created, they are stored as separate image files in one of the above Web formats. Therefore, a document which incorporates an image must contain not only the image *tag* but also the *location* of where that image file is stored. The `src` attribute is the image equivalent of the `href` attribute and the syntax is identical to that of `href`. Here is an example:

Text with an Image

Here we see the Great Crested Geek bird at home in a London marsh.

Note the fine crest feathers.

```
<head>
<title>Putting in an image. </title>
</head>
<body>
<center>
    <h1>Text with an Image</h1>
</center>
Here we see the Great Crested Geek bird at home
in a London marsh.
<p>
<img src="geek-bird.gif" />
</p>
Note the fine crest feathers.
</body>
```

Notes:

1. To ensure the image is separated from any other text in the document it has been enclosed within the non-empty

paragraph element, which forces the image to be a stand-alone image. We could have used a `<div>` tag in place of the `<p>` tag.

2. The basic syntax is: `<img src="animage.jpg" />`. The `src` attribute's value contains the location of where the image is stored. In the source code above, we have used a relative URL, consequently, this image is assumed to be in the same directory/folder as the web page itself.

3. For those who may be familiar with HTML, note that in XHTML the empty `<img>` tag must include the forward slash before the closing angle bracket. We need to discuss empty elements now in greater detail.

Empty Elements in XHTML

The forward slash before the closing > bracket in an empty element is a requirement in XHTML but not in HTML. If you recall, we said on page 5 that XHTML requires that all non-empty elements must have a closing tag and empty elements must include a forward slash (/). *Terminated* is the official term for this. In XHTML we can terminate empty tags in one of two ways.

1. Create an end tag, thus:

`<img src = "a url" > </img>`

2. Include the forward slash within the empty tag itself, thus:

`<img src = "a url" />`

The latter is the preferred method, since Method 1 may cause unexpected results on some browsers.

Consequently, we could have created end tags for the `<hr>` & `<br>` tags, thus: `<hr> </hr>` & `<br> </br>`

Previously, we included the slash within the tag itself, thus: `<hr />` and `<br />`. A space was also inserted after the tag name so that all browsers would 'recognise' the syntax. In other words, we followed the recommended Method 2.

Note, too, that a space is included before the slash. This ensures that all browsers will recognise the syntax. Method 2 is sometimes referred to as the *minimised* tag syntax.

Relative Links

If the image file is in the same location as the document then *relative* links may be used. If the file is in a sub-directory of the current directory then the sub-directory needs to be included. If you tend to work with images, it is sometimes more convenient to store them in a sub-folder, for example: `images`. This means that your image files can be kept separate from your web pages.

We are talking about your computer's hard disc where you store your XHTML and images files whilst you are developing your web pages. Eventually, you will have to pass all the files to your Web Manager who will decide exactly where they will be stored on the web server.

```
<img src="images/imagename.gif" />
```

If the image file is stored at a different site, then the full URL must be given:

```
<img
  src="http://www.ic.ac.uk/images/face.gif" />
```

To Align Text with an Image

We should note that the image element is another example of a block element. In the above example, the image was displayed in its own 'surrounding', text above and below but it is possible for text to flow on the same line as the image, for example:

```
<img src="tent.gif" alt="My tent." />
Where to pitch your tent!
<p>Most camping sites provide information
about their facilities.</p>
```

Where to pitch your tent!

Most camping sites provide information about their facilities.

Note how the text is aligned at the *bottom* of the image - this is the default position. See the `align` attribute below for other placements. The `<p>` element forces the rest of the text below the image.

Making an Image a Hyperlink

To turn an image into a hyperlink, simply include the image tag *within* the non-empty anchor tag, `<a>`, thus:

```
<a  href="url">  <img src="url" />  </a>
```

Note that we need two URLs: one for the image tag so that the image can be found and loaded into the *current* document. A second one for the `<a>` tag so that when and if the image is clicked, the appropriate URL can be located and displayed. The URL referenced by the `href` attribute can be any valid URL, such as another image, a normal web document, a news group reference or an e-mail message.

A slight adjustment could make an image and text hyperlinks.

```
<a href="url">
  <img src="url" /> or this text
</a>
```

If we remove the `<img>` tag from the above, we are left with just the text being a hyperlink. Including the `<img>`tag within the anchor element means we have made the image

71

as well as the text a hyperlink to the document referenced in the `href`-url, either of which could be clicked to obtain the file.

Other `<img />` **attributes**

We mention two more attributes here, `alt` and `align`. The `align` attribute is mentioned more for the sake of completeness, since it is rarely used when style sheets are employed. Indeed, the `align` attribute is deprecated (to be phased out). On the other hand, the `alt` attribute is becoming obligatory in XHTML.

`alt="text"`

Some readers do not wish to display images in order to speed up display. Many browsers allow an option to turn off *'the display of images'* - this is not an uncommon ploy especially when people have slow connections. So what do these people see?

They will see whatever text you have typed in double quotes as the value of the `alt` (*alternative*) attribute, thus:

```
<img
   src="http://www.ic.ac.uk/images/mydog.gif"
   alt="My name is Fritz." />
```

It is a matter of courtesy to let those in the above situations know what they are missing. So in place of the image, they see your text. (Some browsers actually display this text until the image file is finally loaded into the document or when the mouse is moved over the image. In the above example, when someone moves the mouse over the image of my dog, my dog's name will be displayed.)

> *Tip:* You should always include the `alt` attribute in the image element so that should your web page ever have to be rendered on a non-visual browser, that browser can cope, somehow, with the fact that it cannot display images. XHTML requires this attribute to be present.

`align="position"`

In HTML version 2, the *position* values are *top*, *bottom* or *middle*. It specifies the alignment of any accompanying text. Since these are to be deprecated, apart from the fact that they caused somewhat ugly results, we shall not discuss them in this text. For those who do need to know about them and any other deprecated elements and attributes mentioned elsewhere, try my book on HTML: "How to create pages for the Web using HTML", 2nd Edition, in this Babani series.

To overcome the problem of ugly pages using the earlier position values of `top`, `middle` and `bottom`, HTML version 3 included two new values for the `align` attribute `right` & `left`. These attributes refer to the position of the *image* (not the text as with the version 2 values). Images were always left justified in version 2.

```
<img src="images/face.gif" align="right" />
Quite a long sentence but which will wrap to
the left of the image since we have aligned
the image on the right.
```

Quite a long sentence but which will wrap to the left of the image since we have aligned the image on the right.

Note: *The align attribute is deprecated in favour of the style sheet* `float` *property, see page 181. To maintain compatibility with both HTML and XHTML, many authors use the align attribute and the float property. Style sheet properties will always override an attribute when both are present.*

Warning when using `align="left"|"right"`

If you have tried out either of these values, you may have noticed that *all* subsequent text and even small images will wrap on the left or right of the image. I am frequently asked on courses: "How can I get just some of the text wrapped and force the rest to appear below the image?"

There are three methods. The first is to use a `table` but this is not discussed until Chapter 17. A second method is to use style sheets, but this is not discussed until Part 2. So, for the time being, we can use the `<br />` tag with the `clear` attribute value set to "all".

`<br clear="all" />`   *the clear attribute is deprecated!*

This will ensure that everything which follows the break tag moves below the image. You can also use a `left` and a `right` value for the `clear` attribute but they will work only when the value of the image's `align` attribute is the same. It is safer to use the `all` value, then it does not matter how the image is aligned.

The `border` **Attribute**

If you have inserted an image and made it a hyperlink, you may have noticed that a ghastly blue border surrounds the image. Browsers do that to show that it is a hyperlink, in the same way that they turn text into blue and underline it. Worse still is the purple border that some browsers put on a visited link. It is simple to remove this border. Use the `border` attribute of the image tag and set its value to 0. This tells the browser to push the image up to the border, effectively preventing the blue border from becoming visible.

`<img src="rose.gif" border="0" />`

Warning: *The border attribute is deprecated in favour of the border-width style sheet property, see page 173.*

Note: For those familiar with HTML, numerical values were seldom quoted. However, remember that XHTML requires all values to be quoted.

Resizing Images

There are two more attributes we can discuss, the `width` and the `height`. These specify the size, in pixels, of the image's width and height.

```
<img src="url"  width="190" height="256" />
```

You would have to be pretty good at arithmetic to ensure that any revised proportions will not distort the image when you decide to alter its original size. You should also be aware that enlarging or reducing an image will inevitably result in loss of the original quality.

You should either decide on the exact image size within whatever image processing program you are familiar with, for example Adobe PhotoShop, or, for a quick fix, resize the image within Microsoft's Internet Assistant.

Using Internet Assistant

If you open a file with an `htm` extension in Microsoft Word which has Internet Assistant[1], the page is displayed by Internet Assistant rather than the normal Word program. Internet Assistant is a browser but, in Office 97, it has limited capabilities.

In Internet Assistant, an image can be clicked to show re-sizing handles. Using one of the *corner* handles and dragging will enlarge or reduce the image without destroying its proportions.

When you click the *View* menu you will see *HTML Source*. If you select this, you are returned to your source code to

---

[1] A quick way to discover whether your version of Word has Internet Assistant installed, is to open a new document. Then click on the *File* menu. If you can see *Save as HTML*, it has been installed.

discover that Internet Assistant has obligingly added the width and height attributes together with their pixel values.

Warning: *When you select* HTML *Source, Internet Assistant will add a few <meta> tags to your original source. It also has the annoying habit of reformatting the line lengths of your original code by converting to full justification. If you do not want this to happen, create a simple web page which includes the image. Proceed as above but simply make a note of the new width and height values and type them into your own unadulterated source code.*

Also, make certain that the image is not a hyperlink, otherwise when you click it, Internet Assistant will fetch whatever the href *attribute points to. You will be unable to get to the re-sizing handles.*

Image Formats

There are many different formats for storing digital images. Each has advantages and disadvantages. At the present time, web browsers are able to recognise just a few of these formats. Thus, any image to be inserted in a document should conform to one of these formats: GIF, JPEG or PNG.

GIF

Graphics Interchange Format - with a `.gif` filename extension. It is a format which all graphical web browsers can recognise. It is especially useful if the graphical image is a logo, an icon or a banner, where there is little variation in colour detail. It can store black-and-white, greyscale and colour images, although it is limited to 256 colours per image. It is also useful when *transparent* images are required. This allows any background colour on the web page to show through the transparent areas. It also allows for *interlacing*. Usually, images are built up pixel line by pixel line starting at the top and working to the bottom. Interlacing is a technique whereby groups of lines are displayed, interspersed throughout the image, so that the entire image is seen in more and more detail giving the viewer an overall 'picture' of the image from the outset.

JPEG

Joint Photographic Experts Group is a format especially designed for storing photographic images. Its file extension is `.jpeg` or `.jpg`. It has a 24-bit colour depth and should be used when a high level of colour and detail must be preserved, for example with photographs.

Generally, speaking, JPEG format is better than GIF for photographic images. The quality is better and through its more sophisticated compression techniques the resulting files are smaller than an equivalent GIF version.

When saving an image in JPEG format, some image programs allow a *progressive* option to be chosen. It is the equivalent of the GIF interlaced format.

PNG

The last format we shall mention is the Portable Network Graphic (`.png`). Like GIF, it allows for transparency, interlacing and image compression. It has better colour quality than GIF so why have I given up on using `png` images? The problem is that Navigator and IE tend to show the colours differently. The same image often looks much darker in IE than in Netscape, to the extent that the detail becomes blurred. Try it out and make up your own mind.

Adding an Image as a background to a web page

Via the `body` element, we can apply an image as a background to an entire page, using the `background` attribute whose value must be an image file.

```
<body background="image.gif">
```

We saw on page 50 that the `body` tag can also take the `bgcolor` attribute. What happens when both are used?

The `background` image will always take precedence over the `bgcolor`. In other words, the image will sit on top of the coloured background. However, if the image has any transparent areas or is oval in shape within a transparent box, then the background colour will be able to show through.

If the image is smaller than the web page, browsers will *tile* the image so that it fills the entire window. (Using style sheets we can restrict the tiling to a single horizontal or vertical plane.)

Loading Images

a) The browser first retrieves the document itself and displays the text leaving spaces for any `<img>` elements it comes across. It then makes further connections to the Internet to fetch copies of the image files. Thus a document with five images requires six separate connections to the server, one for the original document, then five more trips for each image file. This is clearly time-consuming before the complete document and its five images can be fully displayed.

b) Images which have been scanned using one of the many available scanners are frequently saved in a non-web format. I usually save all my scanned images in TIFF (Tagged Image File Format) because it is an industry standard and saves the image in high quality. All image processing programs can open a TIFF image. These programs can then be used to touch up the image and to save it in a GIF, JPG or PNG format.

c) When an image is loaded, most browsers will store the image in a *cache* memory (a part of your hard disc). If the image is required again, perhaps because it is repeated on the same page, for example a repeated image used as a bullet, or perhaps because the user re-sizes the window thus forcing the browser to reload (re-display) the entire page again, the image can be retrieved from the cache memory rather than the browser having to retrieve yet another copy over the Internet. This clearly speeds up the screen's re-painting process.

d) Whenever practical, always include the *width* and the *height* attributes. (Indeed, it may become an XHTML requirement in the future.) When they are present, the browser will allocate the correct space for the image and display the *alt* attribute's *value* until the image is loaded. If the size attributes are not present, some space is allocated for the image but since its actual size is not known, the entire page will have to be repainted once the image does arrive. In other words, you slow down the eventual page display when the *width* and *height* attributes are not present but can speed up the display when they are present.

e) Although it was quite obvious once it had been pointed out to me, I had not given much thought to exactly what the `width` and `height` attributes of the `img` tag actually do. Say you have an original image file of 50K bytes. You reduce its size exactly by half using the attributes above. This does not speed up the *delivery* of the original file. The original 50K will still have to travel over the Internet. Then once it has arrived, the browser will fit the original into the space you have allocated. In other words, the original will not be reduced to 25K until it is processed by the browser, so it will still take the same amount of time to arrive.

What you have learnt

You have learnt how to incorporate images into your web pages; how to wrap text around the image; how to convert an image into a hyperlink.

You should now be able make your web pages much more attractive.

We also went into detail about how XHTML treats empty elements.

Summary of XHTML Elements covered in Chapters 6 - 7

XHTML tag	Attributes
`<a>...` `</a>`	href = "url" name="venue" - place to move to in a document
`<body>..` `</body>`	background - tile an image on web page bgcolor - colour web page background
` `	clear = left I right I all. It is safer to use *all*
`<img />`	align - left I right alt - alternative text to display for image height - in pixels height of image width - in pixels width of image src = "url" of where image is stored

Converting to XHTML

Requirement	Example

Empty tags, such as `<img>` require an end tag `</img>` or, a forward slash before the closing > bracket. The latter is recommended in preference to the closing tag.	`<img src="url"`
	   `alt="some text" />`
	
	Note the space before the slash. This ensures backward compatibility.

Test

1. What `img` attribute is required to display an image within a web page?

2. If the image you want loaded is stored at some external site, what would happen if that site moved the image to some other folder without telling you?

3. Let us say that you see a web page with your organisation's logo on it. You would like to use it on your own web pages and have been given permission to do so. How would you obtain a copy of that logo?

4. You see a picture on someone else's web site and would like to use it for your own web page. The answer to the

above question tells you how simple it is to obtain that image. But could you be in breach of copyright?

5. You have made an image a hyperlink, but are now dismayed to find that a horrible blue line runs around the entire image box. It looks even worse after it is clicked because now the browser puts a *purple* border around the image. How can you get rid of the border?

6. How can you tell whether you have Internet Assistant in your Word program?

7. What is wrong with this?

```
<img src=some.jpg>
```

8: Summary of XHTML Syntax

We have seen enough XHTML elements by now to be in a position to summarise the syntax of XHTML. There are some features of the syntax which relate to `forms`, `tables` and image *hot spots* which we have yet to discuss. Therefore, some of the elements and attributes may not be known to you, but they are noted here for later enlightenment.

After the summary we shall look at the purpose and meaning behind those first few lines of code which we have been inserting in our XHTML documents, the so-called *declaration*.

First, we need to understand the connection between XML and XHTML?

XML & XHTML - the Connection

XML is a meta language which simply means that it is used to describe other languages. XML was used to describe (*define* if you prefer) the XHTML language. Therefore, the XHTML syntax has been defined by XML. In a way, it is like referring to English grammar as the 'language' I use in this book. In order to write all these sentences, and, I trust, make sense to those of you who read it, I must follow the rules or syntax of English grammar. This book, then, can be thought of as an *instance* of English grammar. It is not the English language as such, rather it is an example of what can be written using the grammar of the English language.

In order to write an XHTML web page, we need to follow the rules (grammar, syntax, take your pick) of XML. Each XHTML web page we create is an *instance* of XML.

HTML, on the other hand, was defined according to the rules of an earlier meta language called SGML (Standard Mark-up Language). Every HTML web page is an instance of SGML but a very simple sub-set of SGML. Why it became necessary to move from SGML to XML (really HTML to XHTML) is discussed in detail in Chapter 21.

Briefly, however, SGML is a very powerful language, but it is also the 'mother of all complexity'. SGML was seen to be too complex to develop HTML any further. So, a simpler version of SGML was developed, XML, to define XHTML - a new web language for the needs of today. It has 80% of the power of SGML, but only 20% of its complexity.

For the purpose of this Chapter, we simply need to know that web pages written in XHTML are based on the syntax of the XML language rather than the syntax of SGML used for HTML. Therefore, in order to understand the syntax of XHTML we need to look briefly at the syntax of XML.

XML Syntax
XML is a simple meta language with very few rules.

- case is significant
- XML documents must be well-formed

A well-formed document is one which follows these rules:

- all elements must have matching opening and closing tags
- empty elements must be written in a special way
- all elements must be properly nested
- there must be a single *root element* that contains all the other elements

The XHTML Syntax

Apart from the above, XHTML has a few extras of its own which relate directly to pages created for the WWW. In the following, the terms *elements*, *opening* and *closing tags* and *content* have the meaning described on page 19. There are ten points to discuss.

1. Mandatory tags

The `<head>` and `<body>` elements must not be omitted and, furthermore, the `<title>` element must be the first element after the opening `<head>` tag. The `<html>` element is also mandatory but is discussed under the *root* element below.

2. Tag and attributes names must be in lowercase

This results from XML being case sensitive.

HTML	XHTML
`<BODY BGCOLOR="teal">`	`<body bgcolor="teal">`
`<P> A new paragraph.` `</P>`	`<p> A new paragraph.` `</p>`
`A <B>bold</B> word`	`A <b>bold</b> word`

We can no longer get away with putting tag names in uppercase to aid readability.

3. Elements must nest, not overlap

Most browsers have been taught to tolerate sloppy HTML code, but this meant that the browser program had to have much more programming code to take our bad habits into account. The new Internet devices will not have the memory capacity to cope with such large programs which also require more processing time when they have to 'guess' at what was really intended. For example, what do I really intend to do in the following?

`<h2>a <i>heading </h4> </i>`

It is quite a mess - different heading levels and incorrect nesting. One browser's 'interpretation' of what I meant to do would not necessarily be the same as another browser's 'interpretation'.

> *A tolerant browser will ignore the errors even, for the time being, an XHTML compliant browser. That is why, if your XHTML code is incorrect, it will still work on many browsers. See Chapter 20 to discover how you*

can check whether your XHTML source code is indeed syntactically correct.

With the advent of different Internet devices[1], such as talking car phones, TV boxes, small palm top computers, they will not have the same processing power as a typical desk top computer. Consequently, one of the aims of XHTML was that the source code must be rigid in its syntax, in order to reduce the program size to fit into the smaller devices.

HTML	XHTML
`<p> Here is a <b>bold phrase <i> followed by a bold italic phrase. </p> </b> </I>`	`<p> Here is a <b>bold phrase <i> followed by a bold italic phrase. </i> <b> </p>`

In XML all elements must be correctly nested. If not, and this applies to the other rules of syntax, the user agent (the browser) is under no obligation to continue displaying the page. This will not affect us for the moment, but come the day when smaller devices are being used, your web page will no longer be rendered.

The term render *is used by W3C to include user agents capable of visual, aural and printed presentation.* Display *is reserved solely for visual presentation.*

4. All non-empty elements must be closed

All elements, non-empty and empty, must be closed.

HTML	XHTML
`<p> In classic HTML we seldom bothered to use a closing paragraph tag, list tag, table data tag, and many more.` `<p>But now we must.`	`<p> In classic HTML we seldom bothered to use a closing paragraph tag, list tag, table data tag, and many more.</p>` `<p>In XHTML we must.</p>`

---

[1] These devices, including PCs and MACs, capable of rendering XHTML code are known as *user agents* by the W3C Consortium.

Here are some of the common ones which were seldom closed in HTML, but which *must be closed* in XHTML:

```
<li>  <p>  <th>  <td>  <tr>  <dd>  <dt>  <html>
<option>  <div>
```

5. Empty Elements must be Terminated - Closed
This is probably something quite new to those of us familiar with HTML. Empty elements, such as `<hr>`, `<br>` and `<img>` which have no content and consequently no closing tag, must be terminated. XML, and therefore our XHTML source code, requires a trailing forward slash (`/`) before the end bracket. (See also page 69.)

To maintain compatibility with non-XHTML compliant browsers, it is advisable to add a space before the slash.

HTML	XHTML
`<IMG src="fritz.gif"` `    alt= "some text">`	`<img src="fritz.gif"` `    alt= "some text" />`

`<HR>`
`lines of text`
`<HR>`
	`<hr />`
	`lines of text`
	`<hr />`

`John Smith  ` `ABC Ltd.  ` `jsmith@abc.org  `	`John Smith  ` `ABC Ltd.  ` `jsmith@abc.org  `

Other affected empty elements are:

```
<meta>  <input>  <area>  <link>
```

6. Attribute Values must be Quoted
Every value must be quoted in either double or single quotes. Even numeric values, seldom quoted in HTML, must now be quoted. Note also how we have included the `alt` attribute in the XHTML version of the `<img>` tag since this is now a required attribute. We have also used single and double quoted values to remind you that either is acceptable.

HTML	XHTML
`<img src = "mydog.gif" border=0>`	`<img src = "mydog.gif" alt = 'Called Fritz' border= "0" />`

7. Attributes cannot be Minimised

In classic HTML some attributes took the same value as the attribute name. For example, `<ul>` and `<dl>` can take the `compact` attribute which simply asks for the content to be displayed in a more compact, i.e. smaller, font. Thus:

```
<dl compact="compact">
```

This could be shortened to:

```
<dl compact>   ... In HTML
<dt> Term to be defined </dt>
<dd> The actual definition </dd>   </dl>
```

The above is pure HTML and was called *attribute minimisation* where the *value* is the same as the *attribute name*. Well, that cannot be done any more. We have to forgo the shorter (minimised) method in favour of the long method. Here are some other examples, using attributes associated with `forms` and `tables`.

HTML	XHTML
`<ul compact>`	`<ul compact="compact">`
`<option .... selected>`	`<option .... selected="selected">`
`<input type="radio" checked>`	`<input type="radio" checked="checked" />`
`<td nowrap>`	`<td nowrap="nowrap">`

8. The Root Element

XML requires that there must be a special element which encloses the whole body of the document. It is known as the *root element*. This is to allow the browser to recognise when the document has been completely read. In other words, this root element marks the beginning and end of the *entire* XML document. Since an XHTML document is an XML document, it too must have a root element.

In XML, an author may invent any name for the root element, but in XHTML, this root element must be `<html>`. Furthermore, the opening root tag must designate the XHTML *namespace*, thus:

```
<html xmlns="http://www.w3.org/1999/xhtml">
```

We shall dissect this below. For the moment, we simply need to know that this special root element is mandatory and must be the `<html>` element.

9. Whitespace handling in attribute values

Within an attribute *value*, all whitespace (tabs, line breaks, extra spacing) will be stripped out and replaced by a single inter-word space.

10. Elements with `id` and `name` attributes

Both these attributes were introduced into HTML 4. However, the `name` attribute is deprecated and will be removed from future versions of XHTML. For the present time, XHTML 1.0 (the only version in existence at the time of writing) allows both to be used to ensure backward compatibility with non-XML browsers.

So, what is this `id` attribute? It is used to replace the `name` attribute and is used with style sheets. So we shall leave any further discussion until Part 2.

Those first Few Lines - the Declaration

In Chapter 1, we simply stated that all XHTML documents must have the following three elements inserted:

```
<?xml version="1.0" encoding="UTF-8"?>
<!DOCTYPE html
PUBLIC "-//W3C//DTD XHTML 1.0 Transitional//EN"
      "http://www.w3.org/TR/xhtml1/DTD/
       xhtml1-transitional.dtd">
<html xmlns="http://www.w3.org/1999/xhtml"
      xml:lang="en" lang="en">

      everything else ..... goes here ....
</html>
```

It is now time to find out what they are all about and why we need them. There are three lines in the declaration.

1. The version declaration
The first is:

```
<?xml version="1.0" encoding="UTF-8"?>
```

This simply states that we are using version 1.0 of XML (the only one at the time of writing) and is called the *version declaration.* In XML, this begins with `<?xml` and ends with `?>` Note the question marks.

By now we should not be surprised that our XHTML document is an instance of an XML document. So what we are really telling our browser is that it has met an XML document.

The second attribute specifies which character encoding set is to be used for the document. It is UTF-8 which is the default value and the one used for standard English. It stands for UCS Transformation Format using an eight-bit code. UCS stands for Universal Character Set.

> *I used to think that typing the letter 'a' on a keyboard and having it stored inside my computer would be comparatively simple. In practice, it is a highly complex affair. If you want to see just what is involved, try this site, current at the time of writing:*
>
> `http://www.hut.fi/u/jkorpela/chars.html`
>
> *If this fails, try Ask Jeeves by typing in* character sets *in the search engine search box.*

Strictly speaking, this declaration tag is not a requirement, in XHTML 1.0, but W3C *strongly encourages* its use in all XHTML documents. The reason for this is that the declaration also specifies the character set to be used. If you were using a language with other character requirements, such as Japanese, then the encoding attribute must be used with the relevant value pointing to the Japanese character set. In this case, the entire element would be required.

2. The DTD Declaration

```
<!DOCTYPE html
PUBLIC "-//W3C//DTD XHTML 1.0 Transitional//EN"
    "http://www.w3.org/TR/xhtml1/DTD/
            xhtml1-transitional.dtd">
```

This second element specifies the DTD (Document Type Definition) to be used via the DOCTYPE declaration. It is a requirement that all XHTML documents are validated (checked for correct syntax) by a DTD. The DTD is identified by the PUBLIC identifier. (Do note the use of uppercase. These first two elements do not form part of XHTML.)

What is a DTD?
SGML introduced the concept of a DTD and it has been carried forward into XML. It is simply a formal definition of what a document can and cannot contain. You can think of a DTD as being a set of rules that describes what is allowed and what is not allowed in an XML document. Since XHTML is an instance of an XML document, it too requires a DTD, a separate document which defines how the mark-up tags should be interpreted by the browser.

Each element in an XHTML document is compared against the DTD to see what sort of tag it is and what the browser must do with it. If a tag is not in the DTD, then it is invalid. What the browser then does depends on the 'whim' of the browser manufacturer. If you become involved in writing XML documents, you may then have to create your own DTDs. But as far as we are concerned, the DTD for XHTML has already been written for us by the W3C. Our duty is simply to include a reference to it. There are, in fact, three versions.

Browsers have programs called *parsers* which perform the validation of our web page against one of three DTDs:

- Strict
- Transitional
- Frameset

For an XHTML document to conform to standard XHTML, it must be validated against one of the above three DTDs. The *strict* version can be thought of as the core set of elements and attributes in XHTML.

```
<!DOCTYPE html
   PUBLIC "-//W3C//DTD XHTML 1.0 Strict//EN"
         "http://www.w3.org/TR/xhtml1/DTD/
            xhtml1-strict.dtd">
```

Note that the PUBLIC identifier (an SGML attribute) contains two pieces of information each enclosed in double quotes. The first identifies which DTD the browser must use (*Strict* in the example below):

```
"-//W3C//DTD XHTML 1.0 Strict//EN"
```

the second gives the web address of where to find the file:

```
"http://www.w3.org/TR/xhtml1/DTD/
            xhtml1-strict.dtd"
```

The *transitional* version includes all the strict tags and attributes plus some extras. For example, `<dir>` and `<menu>` which are not in the Strict DTD. This allows for backward compatibility with browsers which can only recognise classic HTML.

```
<!DOCTYPE html
PUBLIC "-//W3C//DTD XHTML 1.0 Transitional//EN"
      "http://www.w3.org/TR/xhtml1/DTD/
            xhtml1-transitional.dtd">
```

The Frameset DTD is identical to the Transitional DTD except that it includes two extra elements used with frames, `<frame>` and `<frameset>`. So, if you are using frames in your web page, then you must choose this DTD. See Appendix B for a summary of the Transitional and Frameset DTD.

```
<!DOCTYPE html
PUBLIC "-//W3C//DTD XHTML 1.0 Frameset//EN"
      "http://www.w3.org/TR/xhtml1/DTD/
              xhtml1-frameset.dtd">
```

Do note the mix of case throughout this element. That is why you were advised to create a blank template so that you will not make typing errors. But which of the three should you go for? Some advise the Strict DTD because many of the additional elements and attributes in the other two are likely to be phased out in later versions of XHTML, i.e. they are *deprecated*. I personally use the Transitional DTD since this makes my web pages backward compatible with older browsers. The Frameset DTD must be used if you include frames. We do not discuss frames in this text since they are deprecated in XHTML in favour of style sheets.

3. The `<html>` Element

Finally, we look at the third element.

```
<html xmlns="http://www.w3.org/1999/xhtml"
                  xml:lang="en" lang="en">
```

If you recall from point 8 above, all XML documents must contain a *root* element which encloses all the other elements. When an XML document is an XHTML document, this *root* must be the `<html>` element and must come after the previous two elements. All three must be placed before the `<head>` element, in the order given.

Since we are talking about order, the attributes in the first two elements are order dependent!

Since the `<html>` element is part of XHTML, the element and the attributes must be in lowercase.

There are three pieces of information in the root element.

```
xmlns="http://www.w3.org/1999/xhtml"
```

This first is the `xmlns` attribute which stands for 'XML namespace'. So, what is a *namespace*?

The XML Namespace

Every element and attribute in an XML document belongs to a *namespace*. A namespace is simply a list of all the elements which can be used. However, the namespace is required to have a unique name. In XHTML, the namespace is declared via the `xmlns` attribute within the `<html>` element. The value of the `xmlns` attribute must be a unique name to identify the namespace. It was decided to use a URI (Uniform Resource Identifier) for this name since like any address or telephone number, it is unique.

All we really need to know is that we must include the namespace within our XHTML documents via the `xmlns` attribute. The XML namespace is a list of all valid elements which can be used in our XHTML documents. (For the more technically minded, there is a reference to an article about XML namespaces in Appendix A by Lisa Rein.)

`xml:lang` & `lang` Attributes

The other two attributes are `xml:lang` and `lang`. Both should be used for backward compatibility. The value of each is `"en"` for English. `xml:lang` is for XHTML compatible browsers; `lang` is the classic HTML language attribute. Here are some other values which refer to different languages.

`"en"`	English
`"en-US":`	the U.S. version of English.
`"en-cockney":`	the Cockney version of English.
`"fr"`	French
`"de"`	German
`"it"`	Italian
`"nl "`	Dutch
`"el "`	Greek
`"es"`	Spanish
`"pt"`	Portuguese
`"ja"`	Japanese

Part 2

Cascading Style Sheets

In this section, we shall see how style sheets can bring desk top publishing to our Web pages. We shall discuss the syntax of CSS and note that it is a different language to XHTML. Therefore we shall have to learn a new syntax.

We shall see how to create:

- white space margins without using tables
- drop caps
- shadow effects
- first line indents
- small caps
- outdented headings
- line spacing and letter spacing
- a border around paragraphs

In addition, we shall see:

- how to add a background image as a single vertical or horizontal column/row and to fix an image with text scrolling over it
- how to absolutely position text and images
- how to change point sizes and typeface for text
- how to colour text and add a background colour to block elements
- how to float text around images
- how to overlap text and images
- how to make text invisible

We shall discuss the *parent-child inheritance* and why the term *cascading* is used.

9: Introduction to CSS

Why Bother with CSS?

There are so many advantages to style sheets that it is difficult to know where to begin. However, one of the most important, for me at any rate, is that one can separate content from style. So let us begin with that.

Content versus Presentation

The original intention behind HTML was to permit academics and researchers to pass information over the WWW in a simple manner via hyperlinks. The content had a simple and basic structure but without any fancy formatting. Thus, there were levels of headings, paragraph tags, simple list and blockquote tags. That is all it was designed for. It did not catch on. Images were included in HTML 1 and it did catch on and to a much wider audience.

The new audience, however, were hungry for new tags and attributes which would make their web pages more attractive. So, Netscape introduced the `<center>` tag and Microsoft went mad with alignment, colour, typeface attributes. The end result is that HTML source code contains so many tags and attributes that the content is difficult to read, let alone amend. Worse, some browsers do not recognise some of the tags and attributes 'invented' by other browser manufacturers, so that a web page can be displayed differently depending on which browser is being used. For Web authors, this has been a nightmare resulting in many web pages having to start off by saying something like: *"This page is best viewed in Browser ABC version 1.3."*

Now, imagine a Web where there are no proprietary tags and where web authors have complete control over the presentation of their pages. That is the promise of CSS.

We can use XHTML to create the content of our web pages and we can use a different technology, CSS, to present that content.

Here are some of the reasons why we might want to separate content from its style.

1. The XHTML source code is cleaner making it easier to read and amend when it is no longer littered with presentational tags and attributes.

2. One person can concentrate on the content and the arty person can concentrate on its presentation.

3. Organisations can provide a house-style for all their web pages by linking the XHTML source code to an external style sheet. (See page 107 for linking to external style sheets.)

In summary, separating the presentational aspects of documents from their content simplifies Web authoring and site maintenance. Style sheets make this separation easy.

Different Internet Access Devices

According to many computer analysts, it is expected that by the year 2002 70% of Internet access will be via devices other than our home/office PCs and MACs. TV Internet boxes, small palm top computers, talking car phones and, dread the day, talking mobiles, are just some of these devices. But there are others, such as devices for the blind whereby special sound-oriented style sheets could specify speech parameters, intonation, and so on. There is even talk, as yet, of *feelie* devices as well as devices which will belch out smells!

By separating the style from the content, it will be easier to adapt the content to these other devices. [1]

There is also a growing demand for multi-media content and e-commerce. HTML was not designed for such heady excitement. It prefers the simple life, hence the need for new and more vibrant web languages such as XHTML and CSS. Our browsers will need to be able to recognise both of these recent technologies.

DTP meets the Web

HTML is not that good at presentation but it was never intended to be. Over the past few years many attempts have been made to improve the appearance of web pages; colour, choice of typefaces, animated graphics via JavaScript, and so on. But it is still not quite desk top publishing (DTP). CSS is changing that. By using style sheets, we can bring many DTP features to our web pages. For instance we can choose point sizes for our text, not just rely on relatively larger or smaller text which the `size` attribute permits. We can precisely set margins rather than having to resort to `tables`. Letter and word spacing, line spacing, drop caps, superimposing one text over another, are some of the other features which we shall be looking at in the coming chapters. In fact, via CSS, we are fast approaching the sophistication of DTP.

Adding New Features

Adding new tags to HTML was not simple. It took several years before Netscape's `<center>` tag could be universally adopted. Likewise for the `<font>` element, which HTML relies on for many presentational features. Making new additions to either XHTML or CSS will be a much easier and faster process.

---

[1] The W3C technical term for all these devices is *User Agents*. These encompass screen, aural and printed media.

99

Now the Bad News

After all the above excitement, and as we are all itching to get to grips with CSS, we find that few browsers support it, and those that do have not implemented all of its features. At the time of writing, December, 2000, Internet Explorer version 5 supports many features, but not all. Netscape version 4 has a half-hearted approach to CSS which means that few of the features actually work. Opera, is the only browser (to my knowledge) which not only implements most (some claim all) of CSS but has also tested it thoroughly before releasing it. But, they have implemented CSS1, not, at the time of writing, CSS2. Matters are improving, and perhaps by the time you read this book, the then current browsers may well support many of the features covered here.

We shall examine CSS version 1 and 2 in this text. Where possible, I will point out which features work with IE5 and Netscape 4.5. We need to know all the features now so that when all the features are implemented we shall be ready to use them. I strongly advise you to try out your styles in both IE and Netscape so that you can see which work and which do not. Despite these difficulties, I am still a fan. It will get better, and the time to start experimenting is now.

Versions of CSS

There are, currently, three versions of CSS, sometimes referred to as levels. At the time of writing, CSS level 3 (CSS3) is still under development.

The Basic syntax of CSS

It is high time that we began to see how to write style sheets. You will need Internet Explorer 5.0 or higher in order to make the most of the features. So, let us make a start with a basic XHTML page.

We shall

- look at the syntax of CSS
- discuss the terminology in use
- write a simple style sheet

My First CSS Exercise

This is a paragraph in point size 12
and in the Comic Sans MS typeface.
The heading will be in the colour teal,
point size 14 and have the default
Times New Roman typeface.

```
<?xml version="1.0" encoding="UTF-8"?>
<!DOCTYPE html
PUBLIC "-//W3C//DTD XHTML 1.0
        Transitional//EN"
"http://www.w3.org/TR/xhtml1/DTD/
        xhtml1-transitional.dtd">
<html xmlns="http://www.w3.org/1999/xhtml"
      xml:lang="en" lang="en">
<head>
<title>First CSS exercise</title>
<style type="text/css">
p {font-family:"comic sans ms";
   font-size:12pt;}
h2 {font-size:14pt; color:teal;}
</style>
</head>
<body>
<h2>My First CSS Exercise</h2>
<p> This is a paragraph in point size 12 and
in the Comic Sans MS typeface. The heading
will be in the colour teal, point size 14 and
have the default Times New Roman typeface.
</p>
</body> </html>
```

Notes:

1. First of all notice how 'clean and uncluttered' the source code within the `<body>` element is. It contains only the content and basic elements.

2. But where are all the formatting instructions? These are within the `<style>` element. A browser which is able to recognise style sheets, reads the style instructions, called *rules*, to see how to display the XHTML elements (just the `<p>` and `<h2>` in our example). Everything between the `<style>` tags is known as a *style sheet*.

3. We must also include the `type` attribute with the value `"text/css"`

```
<style type="text/css">
```

This tells the browser that the style sheet is going to be a CSS style sheet. There are other types of style sheet languages in existence, so this attribute is necessary.

4. In the above style sheet, there is a reference to the paragraph and heading 2 elements. But see how they are written without the angle brackets. CSS is not XHTML nor even XML. It is a separate language, designed in 1996 and has its own syntax. Consequently, we could use uppercase for P and H2. We shall always use lowercase to remain consistent with XHTML. The XHTML elements are called *selectors* when they appear in a style sheet.

5. The styles to apply to the selected XHTML element (the selector) are contained within curly brackets { }. These may be typed on one line (as with the heading 2 element) or on separate lines, as with the paragraph element. It is your choice.

```
p {font-family:"comic sans ms";
   font-size:12pt;}
h2 {font-size:14pt; color:teal;}
```

6. Each style is called a *property* in CSS terminology and each property is given a *value*. Note how a colon is used to separate the property from its value. Note also that each property-value ends with a semi-colon.

```
property:value;
```

The semi-colon is optional on the last property-value pair, i.e. on the last one before the closing curly bracket. Most CSS practitioners would advise that it should always be included. In the next few chapters, we shall look at what properties can be used with XHTML elements and what values those properties can take.

In the above, we use three properties - note the hyphens:

`font-family:` specifies a typeface
`font-size:` specifies a character size
`color:` specifies a text colour (note US spelling)

7. One value has been quoted, the rest have not. Remember, we are using the CSS language here, not XHTML. The syntax for CSS requires that values must *not be quoted* unless they contain whitespace such as `comic sans ms` which has spaces between each word.

If we had quoted "teal", it would not be valid CSS. Just to see what happens, try the above in both IE5 and Netscape. IE5 will give the correct colour, but Netscape 4.5 will often display some other colour. This is another advantage for separating the XHTML content from the CSS style sheets. You can then concentrate on the correct syntax for each language.

Look at Chapter 20 to see how you can check your style sheets for any errors by using the W3C CSS Validator.

Style Rule terminology

Style rules are used to state how the content of a web page is to be displayed. A style rule consists of a *selector* and a *declaration* enclosed in curly brackets.

In the following, `p` is the selector (the XHTML element) and `font-size:12pt;` is the declaration.

`p { font-size:12pt;}` - a complete style rule

A declaration consists of a *property* name and a *value* with a colon separating the two.

If more than one declaration is made within the curly brackets, semi-colons are used to separate each declaration. The final declaration may take an optional semi-colon.

`p {font-size:12pt; color:red;}`

Term	Example
selector, almost any XHTML element without the angle brackets	p h1 div body
declarations - property:value;	{font-size:12pt;}
property name	font-size:
property value	12pt

What you have learnt

We discussed many of the advantages of using style sheets and seen how to write a simple style sheet. It became clear that CSS is a different language to XHTML and as such has its own syntax.

Now that we know the basic syntax of CSS we can look at what properties are available and what values the various properties can take.

Test

1. Which of the following are valid ways of writing style rules?

```
p
{
font-size:10pt; color:red;
}

p {font-size:10pt; color:red;}
```

```
p {font-size:10pt;
   color:red;}
```

2. How many errors can you spot in the following?

a) `H2 (fontfamily=maroon) ( )` - wrong value
b) `p {colour = "red";}` color value not quoted

3. Create a style sheet for one of your XHTML documents.

10: Why the Cascading in CSS ?

In this chapter, we shall see why the word *cascading* is used in CSS and then examine two new attributes namely, *class* and *id*, and see how and why they are used in style sheets.

What we cover

- what *cascading* means
- external style sheets using <link> and @import
- inline styles
- <link>
- the class attribute
- the id attribute

The style sheet used in the previous chapter and enclosed within the `<style>` tags, is not the only way to create style sheets. We can link an *external* style sheet to any of our XHTML documents and we can also make use of the inline `style` attribute with many XHTML elements. Let us discuss external style sheets first.

External Style Sheets

We have mentioned several times now that separating content from the presentational details is one of the many advantages of using style sheets. Via the `<link>` element, placed after the `<title>` element, we can specify a link to a separate style sheet. Here is an example, using the same web document from the previous chapter. It will do exactly the same.

```
<?xml version="1.0" encoding="UTF-8"?>
<!DOCTYPE html
PUBLIC "-//W3C//DTD XHTML 1.0
        Transitional//EN"
        "http://www.w3.org/TR/xhtml1/DTD/
                 xhtml1-transitional.dtd">
```

```
<html xmlns="http://www.w3.org/1999/xhtml"
              xml:lang="en" lang="en">
<head>
<title>First CSS exercise</title>
<link rel="stylesheet"
      type="text/css"
      href="csstest1.css" />
</head>
<body>
<h2>A Linked CSS Exercise</h2>
<p> This is a paragraph in point size 12 and
in the Comic Sans MS typeface. The heading
will be in the colour teal, point size 14 and
have the default Times New Roman typeface.
</p>
</body>
</html>
```

Notes:

1. All that has changed is that the style sheet within the `<style>` element as well as the `style` element have been completely replaced with the `<link>` element. Since it is an empty element and we are writing in XHTML, we need to include the forward slash just before the closing angle bracket. This element must also appear within the `<head>` tags. Finally, the *values* must be quoted since this element forms part of the XHTML language.

```
<link rel ="stylesheet"
      type="text/css"
      href="csstest1.css" />
```

2. It contains three attributes, `rel`, `type` and `href`.

`rel` is used to show the relationship between the current document and the referenced resource specified in the `href` attribute. Since we are referring to a style sheet, we need to use the `stylesheet` value.

`type` tells the browser that it is going to be a CSS type of style sheet.

`href` provides the location address of the style sheet. Note the `css` extension. Here we are using a relative address, therefore, the style sheet file is in the same folder as the XHTML file. If the style sheet document is held elsewhere, then a complete URL (now called a URI - same thing!) must be provided.

That is all we need to do in order to link an XHTML document to an external style sheet. So, why would we want to do it, after all the browser will have to make another trip over the Internet to fetch a copy? Simply, because this could be a house style-sheet. Rather than force web authors to type the house style sheet into every web page they create, they can simply make a link to the external file.

Another reason, is that Web Masters can tinker around with the external style sheet, confident that all web pages linked to their style sheet will have the latest alterations. (You may not like the idea, but control freaks love it.)

How to Create External style Sheets

Here is the complete external style sheet, saved as: `csstest1.css` It must have the .`css` extension.

```
p   {font-family:"comic sans ms";
     font-size:12pt;}
h2 {font-size:14pt; color:teal;}
```

All we have done is to remove the `<style>` tags and saved the file as a text only file with the appropriate .`css` extension. That is all there is to it. It is tiny, as you can see, so it will travel over the Internet very quickly.

You now know how to copy and paste any style sheet embedded in a web page and how to convert it into an external style sheet which could then be used, via the `<link>` element, in all your web pages. But be careful to remove the `style` tags, because most browsers reading an external style sheet which has `style` tags will simply ignore the style rules entirely.

The @import method

Another way of importing an external style sheet into a web page is via the `@import` statement. However, this method is not fully supported by Netscape 4.

The first step is to create an external style sheet as explained above. It must have a `.css` extension and must not contain any `<style>` tags. Let us suppose that I have created an external style sheet named `housestyle.css`.

The second step is to type the following statement between the `<style>` tags in your XHTML document.

```
<style type="text/css">
@import url("housestyle.css");
p {font-size:12pt; color:teal;}
</style>
```

As you can see, you may also include additional style rules but they must be placed *after* the `@import` statement.

After the `import` statement is the CSS syntax for referencing a `url`. The actual address is typed between the two round brackets. Here we have assumed that the external style sheet is in the same folder as the web page. Should the style sheet be held in some other place, then a complete `url` has to be given:

```
@import url("http://www.abc.com/housestyles/
            housestyle.css");
```

Any web document can now access the style sheet .

> **Note:** *Did you spot the semi-colon at the end of the* `import` *statement? It needs to be present.*

In CSS, the quotes inside the round brackets are optional.

```
@import url(http://www.abc.com/housestyles/
           housestyle.css);
```

The Style Attribute

The fourth way of using style sheets is through the style attribute attached to XHTML elements. Strictly speaking it is not a style sheet but an *inline style attribute*. Here is an example. Suppose I want some text contained within one `<div>` element to be in red and in another to be in blue.

```
<div style = "color:red;">
    some red text goes here </div>
<div style = "color:blue;">
    some blue text goes here </div>
```

As you can see, we are using an inline `style` attribute. Now, be alert! Since this is an XHTML attribute, it must follow the XHTML syntax, not the syntax of CSS.

Consequently, lowercase is used, values are quoted, and we are back to using the `attribute="value"` syntax. The only thing that looks like CSS is the value inside the double quotes. Therefore, note that the *property* is separated from its *value* by the colon: `color:red;` and ends with the semi-colon, just as we did for the CSS style sheet.

We certainly need our wits about us. We sometimes use pure XHTML, sometimes pure CSS and now we have a sort of mixture of the two.

Multiple Inline Style Properties

Suppose we want more than one inline style property. For example, we may want one paragraph of text to be point size 12, red and in Comic Sans MS; a second to be point size 10, teal and in Arial, (the typeface used for most of the paragraphs in this text).

Some Comic Sans Ms text goes here.

Some Arial text goes here.

```
<p style="font-size:12pt;
         color:red;
         font-family:'comic sans ms';">
Some Comic Sans MS text goes here.</p>
<p style="font-size:10pt; color:teal;
   font-family:arial";>
Some Arial text goes here.</p>
```

Notes:

1. All the property declarations are simply enclosed in double quotes, and each declaration ends with a semi-colon.

2. However, do you recall that when a property-value contains white space, it is the one time that CSS requires quotes, either double or single? This is the case with `comic sans ms`, which has spaces. We cannot use a double quote to surround "`comic sans ms`" because we have used the double quote to enclose the entire set of properties. But we still have single quotes in our repertoire. That is why we have surrounded '`comic sans ms`' in single quotes. Now, the browser cannot become confused.

Alternatively, we could have used single quotes to contain all the properties and their values and used double quotes for the `comic sans ms`. The following would be valid.

```
<p style = 'font-size:12pt;
         color:red;
         font-family:"comic sans ms"; '>
Some text goes here.</p>
```

Have you noticed how difficult it is to read the above. We are cluttering up our content with `style` attributes. This is a step backwards, a return to classic HTML. I have tried to make the source code more readable by putting the various properties on separate lines. This is quite valid and is very much a matter of personal style. However, later in this chapter, we shall show how we can avoid the use of the inline *style* attribute by using *id* and *class* attributes instead.

Why the *cascade* in CSS?

We have seen four ways of using CSS. Suppose a web document has a link to an external style sheet, a style sheet enclosed within the style tags (the embedded style sheet) and a few `style` attributes scattered throughout the page. It is valid and not uncommon for all of these methods to be used in web pages. But which will take effect, especially if each one has a different style rule for the same element?

When more than one style sheet exists, it is always the last which will take effect according to the following list:

- external sheets via the link element
- @import external sheets
- embedded style sheets using the style element
- inline style using the style attribute

An inline style, if it exists, will always have the last word. Let us take this example:

We assume that an external style sheet, `csstest1.css` has the following division style:

```
div {font-size:18pt; color:rgb(0,255,0);}
```

An author has created a web page with a link to the external style sheet, the following embedded style sheet and an inline style attribute:

```
<head> <title> ... </title>
<link rel = "stylesheet" type= "text/css"
     href = "csstest1.css" />
<style type="text/css"> /* style sheet */
p {font-size: 20pt;}
</style>
</head>
```

```
<body>
<p style="font-size:15pt;"> <!-- inline -->
First paragraph in 15pt. </p>
<p> Second paragraph in 20pt </p>
<div>A division styled by the external style
sheet in 18pt.</div>
</body>
</html>
```

> First paragraph in 15pt.
>
> ## Second paragraph in 20pt
>
> A division styled by the external style
> sheet in 18pt.

The first paragraph is controlled by the inline style attribute. The second by the embedded style sheet. The division by whatever style was used in the external style sheet.

The term *cascading* refers to the order in which a particular style will prevail. Without any other conflict, an external style sheet will prevail. But if an embedded style rule for the same element is encountered, that will prevail. The effect *cascades* down to the next level. Furthermore, if an inline style attribute is met for the same element, that will take precedence over the embedded style. But do note, that any other paragraphs without a style attribute will now cascade to the embedded style. That is why the second paragraph in the above will be in 20 points.

Style sheet comments

Comments may be added to style sheets and should be used when they can serve some useful purpose. They are enclosed in the following: /* some comment */

```
/* and may spread
over several lines of text */
```

Note how the syntax is different to XHTML comments which use the following:

```
<h2> CEO: James McPhee</h2> <!-- Our CEO will
be leaving in Sept. Replace his name with the
new CEO. -->
```

Author versus the Reader

Some later browsers allow their users to create their own style sheets. This may be important for people with poor sight or a degree of colour blindness, say dark red text on black, or those for whom certain colours result in a migraine. Who now wins, the reader or the author?

Traditionally, CSS1 gave priority to the author. Authors could enforce their style over a reader's style sheet by adding !important to their rule, thus:

```
<style type="text/css">
p {font-size:9pt !important;}
</style>
```

This would override a reader's style sheet even if the reader also has an important designation. However, this was regarded as bad practice and all authors were advised not to use the important designation. Let the reader's style sheet win if it is important to the reader.

> *This has now been reversed in CSS2, so that !important in a CSS2 browser will give priority to the reader, not to the author. Since matters are constantly changing, those of you who wish to remain up-to-date with the changes are referred to the Reference section in Appendix A where some useful web sites, especially that of W3C, are listed.*

As a last point, most browsers allow users to disable style sheets. So in the final analysis, a reader may always win.

The class & id attributes

We finish off this chapter by discussing two attributes, both of which are in HTML 4 and consequently also in XHTML. Let us pose a problem and then see how the `class` attribute can solve it.

Suppose we have three divisions each one containing text which is regarded as having the following priorities: important, normal, low. We would like to indicate each level in a different colour (or font size, or whatever) without resorting to inline style attributes.

```
<style type="text/css">
div {color:red;}
</style>
</head>
<body>
<div> The important priority .. </div>
<div> The normal priority .. </div>
<div> The low priority .. </div>
</body>
```

As the embedded style sheet stands, all three division elements would have their content in red. But by including a *class* attribute within each division, we can refer to one of the divisions via the value of the class attribute.

```
<style type="text/css">
div.red   {color:red;}
div.green {color:green;}
div.blue  {color:blue;}
</style>
</head>
<body>
<div class="red">
 The important priority red .. </div>
<div class="green">
 The normal priority green .. </div>
<div class="blue">
 The low priority blue .. </div>
</body>
```

Notes:

1. Each opening division tag has been given a `class` attribute with a name as its quoted value. Each one can now be referenced independently of any other division by including the class value name in the style sheet.

2. In the style sheet, we have appended each class value to the `div` selector: `div.red`   `div.green`   `div.blue`
In CSS, the selector (`div`) is separated from the class name by a full stop.

3. A `class` attribute and value can be applied to most elements. Thus I may want the contents of a division, a heading level 1 and a paragraph to contain text in red.

```
<style type="text/css">
div.red    {color:red;}
p.red      {color:red;}
h1.red     {color:red;}
</style>
</head>
<body>
<div class="red">
 The division red text .. </div>
<p class="red">
The paragraph red text.. </p>
<h1 class="red">
 The heading red text .. </h1>
</body>
```

Class Value Names

There is a temptation to use names which reflect the formatting style, thus we have used red, green and blue. But a better approach would be to use names which describe the type of content. If red was to be used for any important warning text, a better class value would be warning, important or even red_alert. Any type of warning text, be it a paragraph, a blockquote, division, or whatever, could be given the class value 'warning'. We do so in the following and also show you how the code can be shortened.

```
<style type="text/css">
.warning    {color:red;}
</style>
</head>
<body>
<div class=" warning">
 The division red text .. </div>
<p class=" warning">
 The paragraph red text .. </p>
<h1 class=" warning">
 The heading red text .. </h1>
</body>
```

Notes:

1. The *class selector* (i.e. `.warning`) has no selector (element name). It just follows a full-stop. We could now apply this style rule to any XHTML element which has a `class` attribute with the value `warning`.

2. Sensible class values make the style sheet more meaningful. The above tells us that any text in red must be a warning of some sort. Using the class name `red` gave no meaningful description of the text but now we know it is a *warning* type of text.

Consequently, if we had to add some more "warning" text, say within a blockquote or a level 2 heading, the style sheet could remain unchanged. We would merely have to add `class="warning"` to the opening tag of `<h2>` or `<blockquote>`.

Anyone having to maintain this page, say to add some extra warning text, would be able to interpret the style sheet more easily. The simple name of `red` means very little!

4. There is another way of writing the above:

```
*.warning {color:red;}
```

118

Notice the asterisk (*) preceding the full-stop. This is called the *universal selector* and it simply means 'match any element which contains this class value'.

The id Selector

> # Using the text-indent property
>
> This paragraph will have a 2em first line indent. Try doing that without style sheets!

We can also add an `id` attribute to most XHTML elements. Unlike the `class` attribute's value (the same one can be used many times), the `id` attribute's value must be unique. It can be used only once and is mainly used to uniquely identify one particular element so that it can be manipulated by JavaScript. Let us see an example.

```
<style type="text/css">
#in2em {text-indent:2em; text-align:justify;}
</style>
</head>
<body>
<p id="in2em">
This paragraph will have a 2em first line
indent. Try doing that without style sheets!
</p>
</body>
```

Notes:
1. The `id` attribute must be in lowercase, even in HTML 4. Its value must be unique, so no two `id` attributes can have the same value. This is an important point. It is meant to uniquely identify the use of an element. Consequently, I could not have a second `<p>` with the same `id` value.

119

2. To use the `id` selector in CSS, it must be preceded by the `#` (hash) symbol followed by its value. `#in2em`

3. The style property is `text-indent` (see page 141). Try it out. This is how you can indent the first line of a paragraph.

Advantages of the cascade

An organisation may wish to control the basic style of their web pages. However, an individual department within the organisation may wish to apply certain additional styles of its own. Perhaps they have a particular colour motif. It can do so by embedding its own style sheet (or importing its own style sheet).

Individual members of the Department may also wish to apply their own style on certain pages via embedded style rules (even inline styles if they must). The cascading behaviour of CSS will ensure that their rules will override any others which are external.

> Inline style attributes are not encouraged since they detract from the 'content versus style' approach of XHTML. Should you need to apply style rules for certain elements, use the class and/or id attributes. These still detract from content v. style, but are less obtrusive than the use of style attributes.

What you have learnt

Essentially, we have discussed why the term *cascade* is used with style sheets and we have looked at the various ways in which style can be applied to content. However, there will inevitably be conflicts when one style sheet applies a particular style-property to an element and another style sheet applies a different property to the same element. We have discussed how this conflict is resolved by the cascade sequence.

11: The Font Properties

We have seen enough of the CSS syntax to be able to use style properties. For convenience, the syntax for style rules is summarised below and the properties are divided into categories. The rest of this Chapter discusses the `font` properties.

Style Rule Syntax

- a *style rule* consists of one or more property declarations enclosed in curly brackets and a selector to which to apply the styles
- a *selector* is one of the XHTML elements without the angle brackets
- a *declaration* consists of a property name separated from its value by a colon
- when multiple declarations are included in a rule, each must end with a semi-colon
- the multiple property values for the `font-family` are separated by commas
- values with whitespace must be quoted with either single or double quotes, otherwise values *must not be quoted*

The following illustrates the above syntax:

```
p {font-size:12pt;
   font-family:arial, "comic sans ms",
              sans-serif;}
```

Properties are divided into the following categories:

- **text** properties which control the basic text formatting: case, alignment, indent, line height, spacing and decoration
- **font** properties which control the basic characteristics of a font: typeface, size, small caps, italic, bold
- **color** and **background** properties: Color permits text to be coloured. Background allows a coloured background or an image background to be applied to block elements. An

image background may be repeated, fixed or scrolled and its vertical and horizontal positions may be set

- **box** properties control the margins, padding, borders, width and height as well as the useful floating text property
- **classification** properties which allow elements to be classified, how whitespace is handled, the bullet styles including images for lists, and, the position of list elements

Unhappily, not all the properties are supported as yet. IE5 supports more than Netscape version 4. Opera, it is claimed, supports most of CSS1 properties. However, matters change by the month so I strongly advise all readers to try out their style sheets on as many browsers as possible, certainly on IE and Netscape and to keep returning to the W3C home page to find out what is current. The home page can be found in Appendix A.

The Font Properties
The `font-family` property

font-family	
Value	`[family name, generic name]` `                  |inherit`
Initial	`user agent dependent`
Applies to:	`all elements`
Inherited	`yes`
Percentage	`not available`
Netscape & IE	`implemented in both`

When describing properties, we shall use the above table format which is based on the W3C Specification.

Value: specifies the types of values a property can take. The bar (|) is used to indicate that only one of the values can be selected. The font-family, however, is one of the few properties which can take multiple values. When this occurs, square brackets surround the values.

In the above, font-family names and also a generic name can be given. For example:

```
body {font-family:arial, helvetica,
    "comic sans ms", sans-serif;}
```

The values are in order of priority. The browser is requested to find Arial, if this is not available on the user's machine, to find Helvetica. If this is not available either, then try Comic Sans MS and if all these fail, to get whatever sans serif font is available. The last one is a generic font name, see below.

If you are trying out the CSS validator from W3C and you do not add a generic family, sans serif in the above, you will be given a warning. Authors are advised always to include a generic family as the last value when specific font family names are mentioned.

The inherit value: Each property in CSS2 (not CSS1) may also have a specified value of *inherit*, which simply means that it takes the same property as the element's parent (see page 127). The inherited value is normally used as a fallback value but an author can strengthen its role by setting *inherit* explicitly as a value.

Initial: When a property has not been specified in a style rule, the element takes on some initial or default value. In the case of the font-family, this will be the user agent's choice, usually Times New Roman. User Agent (UA) is a term used by the W3C to refer to the program which is rendering the web page. In our case, the user agent refers to a browser.

Here is the official definition from W3C CSS1 Specification:

"any program that interprets a document written in the document language and applies associated style sheets according to the terms of this specification. A user agent may display a document, read it aloud, cause it to be printed, convert it to another format, etc."

Generic fonts - there are five

serif: those fonts with serifs, such as Times New Roman

sans-serif: those without serifs such as Arial

cursive: such as Zapf-Chancery.

'It is like a hand written script style'

fantasy: these are decorative fonts, no example given

monospaced: such as `Courier New` where each character has the same amount of space whatever its width. For example, although 'w' and 'm' are the widest characters, 'i' and 't' are the thinnest, they will all be given the same space.

Serif and Sans Serif fonts

Look carefully at these two fonts.
The first has little marks on the characters.
These are called *serifs*.

T T

"The River Thames" in a serif font
"The River Thames" in a sans serif font

A sans serif font then, 'sans' being the French for 'without', has no serifs.

Applies to: This section lists the elements to which the property can be applied. All elements are considered to have all properties, but some properties cannot be applied to certain elements. For example, the color property cannot be applied to an `<img>` element and so will have no rendering effect.

Inherited: This states whether the property can be inherited from an element's parent. The `font-family` is a property which can be inherited. Thus, if the `body` element were given the value of Arial, all text elements would inherit this typeface unless explicitly given some other typeface. This is quite useful if you want all your text to be in a certain typeface.

The following would display all text in Arial, except for a `division` block with a class name of `special`.

```
body {font-family:arial, sans-serif;}
div.special {font-family: "times new roman",
                          serif;}
```

percentage: We shall discuss this when we meet a property which can take a percentage value. It has no meaning for the `font-family` property.

Netscape & IE: this is my own addition, not W3C, and it tells you whether the property is implemented in Netscape version 4 and/or IE5.

The `font-style` property
This property essentially allows italics. But it could be used to ask for a normal upright format in a block of text which had previously been set to italic.

font-style	
Value	`normal│italic│oblique│inherit`
Initial	`normal`
Applies to:	`all elements`
Inherited	`yes`
Percentage	`not available`
Netscape & IE	`implemented in both`

```
div {font-style:italic;}
span {font-style:normal;}
```

One of the following three values may be used. The selector may also inherit its parent's font-style value.

normal: is the usual upright style as with this sentence
italic: *slanted letters*
oblique: *also slanted*

Some typeface names include the word Oblique, Slanted or even Incline. Others have Italic, Cursive or Kursiv in their names. By using either oblique or italic, the browser will be able to locate a correct font style based on font names.

`font-variant`
This can be used to create small capital letters, typically for use in a heading. Small-caps are usually a point size smaller than normal uppercase letters.

font-variant	
Value	`normal│small-caps│inherit`
Initial	`user agent dependent`
Applies to:	`all elements`
Inherited	`yes`
Percentage	`not available`
Netscape & IE	`not implemented in Netscape`

```
h2 {font-variant:small-caps;}
```
..... in the style sheet

. . . .

```
<h2>A Heading with Small Caps</h2>
```
.. in the body

would give the following in IE5.

A HEADING WITH SMALL CAPS

```
h1, h2, h3 {font-variant:small-caps;}
```

Here, all headings of levels 1, 2 and 3 will be in small-caps. Note how we can specify all three headings by separating each with a comma. This saves having to type:

```
h1 {font-variant:small-caps;}
h2 {font-variant:small-caps;}
h3 {font-variant:small-caps;}
```

So this is a perfectly valid CSS code:

```
<style type="text/css">
h1, h2, h3 {font-variant:small-caps;}
h1 {color:red;}
h2 {color:green;}
h3 {color:blue;}
</style>
```

All headings will be in small caps, but each level will be in a different colour.

Use of Hyphens

Note that `small-caps` contains a hyphen, as does `sans-serif`, when they are written in a CSS style rule. These are *reserved words* in CSS. Since CSS forbids reserved words to be quoted, it includes the hyphen to prevent the phrase containing whitespace. A value with whitespace must be quoted, but it then becomes a *string*. CSS forbids reserved names to be strings. Therefore, CSS adopted the inclusion of the hyphen to prevent reserved words from being quoted. You will need to remember when to use quotes and when to use hyphens.

`font-weight`
This effectively sets the boldness for text.

font-weight	
Value	normal|bold|bolder|lighter |100|200|300|400|500|600|700 |800|900 |inherit
Initial	normal
Applies to:	all elements
Inherited	yes
Percentage	not available
Netscape & IE	implemented in both

```
span {font-weight:900;}
```

This selects the weight of the font, that is its darkness or how bold it is.

values `100 - 900` form an ordered sequence. Normal is synonymous with 400 and bold is synonymous with 700. Thus, you can work out whether a numerical value is lighter or darker than these norms.

values `normal|bold|bolder|lighter` select font weights which are relative to the weight *inherited* from the *parent*. Now this has opened up a can of worms. Let us digress for a moment to discuss the parent-child relationship and see what a child can expect to inherit from its parent.

Parent-Child Inheritance
Take this simple XHTML document:

```
<?xml version="1.0" encoding="UTF-8"?>
<!DOCTYPE html
       PUBLIC "-//W3C//DTD XHTML 1.0
       Transitional//EN"
      "http://www.w3.org/TR/xhtml1/DTD/
             xhtml1-transitional.dtd">
<html xmlns="http://www.w3.org/1999/xhtml"
      xml:lang="en" lang="en">
<head>
<title>First XHTML exercise</title>
</head>
<body>
<p>A paragraph of text.</p>
</body>
</html>
```

When a browser reads this document it creates a model of all the XHTML elements used. This model reflects the underlying structure of the web page. It is called a *document object model* or DOM. A document contains two main parts, or *objects* as they are called, the version declaration and all the elements and their contents contained within the <html> root element. The main document is called the *parent* of the two children, the *version declaration* and <html>. We are concerned with the root element.

The html element is the parent of two children, a <head> and a <body> element. The <head> is the parent of a child <title> element. The <body> element is the parent of a child <p> element. It is shown in a diagrammatic form on the next page.

Because the <p> element is a child of the <body> element, it will inherit all the properties from its parent, <body>. As we shall see, this is an important factor to bear in mind with some of the properties used in style sheets. Since we have not included a style sheet, the body element will have a default set of properties, typically, font-family Times New Roman, font-size of 12 points, color black, etc.

128

These correspond to the initial values given in our tables. The paragraph element will inherit all these properties from its parent. in other words, the content of the paragraph - "A paragraph of text." - will be displayed in Times New Roman, 12pt and in black.

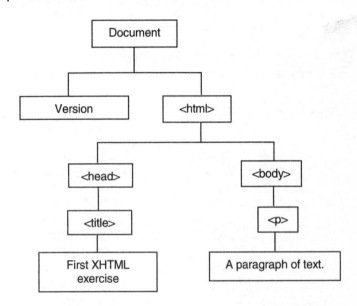

Here is another more complex example which has been saved as `family.htm`.

```
<?xml version="1.0" encoding="UTF-8"?>
<!DOCTYPE html
      PUBLIC "-//W3C//DTD XHTML 1.0
      Transitional//EN"
    "http://www.w3.org/TR/xhtml1/DTD/
            xhtml1-transitional.dtd">
<html xmlns="http://www.w3.org/1999/xhtml"
xml:lang="en" lang="en">
<head>
<title>First XHTML exercise</title>
</head>
```

```
<body>
<p>A paragraph of <b> bold text and <i>
italic </i> </b> text. </p>

<div>Here is a division tag.</div>

<p> <b>Welcome.</b> This is my first XHTML
page.</p>
</body>          </html>
```

Now, rather than draw this diagrammatically, let us get our
IE5 browser to do it for us since this can recognise XML
documents, Netscape 4 cannot.

130

Remember that our XHTML document is an example of an XML document. By replacing the `.htm` extension with a `.xml` extension, we can get IE5 to display it as an XML document. In doing so, it will show the family relationships between all the elements. (See also Chapter 21.)

The result of opening the XHTML file with a `.xml` extension is shown on the previous page. It was originally saved as `family.htm` and re-saved as `family.xml`.

It is a very useful thing to do should you want to see which element belongs to which parent. Instead of the vertical diagram shown above, the *tree,* as it is known, is placed sideways.

Note the minus signs. If you click a minus sign it collapses that part of the tree and the minus is replaced with a plus sign indicating that if clicked it will expand that part of the tree. It also indents the code so that you can see the various levels or parentage more easily.

Thus, following a vertical indent, we can see that the `<body>` is a parent of two `<p>` children and one `<div>` child. All three are at the same level of indentation. The `<div>` has no minus sign, indicating that it has no children of its own. It is simply a child of `<body>`. However, both `<p>` elements have a minus sign and we can now see that the first `<p>` has a `<b>` child which, in turn, is a parent of one child, an `<i>` element. The latter has no children but it does have text.

Text cannot have children. It is the final level and it is this which is actually displayed on the screen. Keeping the tree analogy, this lowest level is called a *leaf.* (Really!)

Why do browsers bother to create such a tree structure? Well, it so happens that tree-structures prove to be a quick and efficient way of organising complex data structures in programming. A browser is a program which has to frequently re-draw (re-paint) the document window each time we, the users, re-size our browser windows. Having all the information about a web document in a tree format makes this process comparatively fast and easy.

The Inheritance

But how will the browser display the text inside the `<i>` tags? Notice how the text belonging to `<i>` is the single word 'italic'. This will clearly be displayed in italic, but it will pick up (inherit) the font size, font family and colour of its parent `<b>`. Of course, through a style sheet rule we could force the colour to be different: i {color:red;}

Given the above rule, the content of `<i>` would now inherit just the font size and font family from its parent.

Going up a level, the `<b>` contains the phrase 'bold text and'. This will be in bold, of course, and will inherit all the properties of its parent, `<p>`. The `<p>` contains two separate phrases, as shown by IE5. These are: 'A paragraph of' and 'text.'. These will inherit the properties of `<p>`'s parent which is `<body>`.

The `<div>` inherits all the properties from its parent - `<body>` and the second `<p>` inherits from its parent which, again, is `<body>`.

So what is all the fuss about? In XHTML, the `<body>` element is the parent of all other elements. By setting properties for the `<body>`, you can apply them to all elements which inherit those properties. It can act as your default set of properties. When other properties are required for particular instances, then these can be added to the style sheet.

```
<style type="text/css">
body {font-family:arial, sans-serif;
      font-size:12pt; color:teal;}
h2   {color:silver; font-size:16pt;}
</style>
```

```
font-size
```
This specifies the font size for text. A font size can be given in many ways:

font-size	
Value	`<absolute>|<relative>|<length>` `|<%>|inherit`
Initial	`medium`
Applies to:	`all elements`
Inherited	`yes`
Percentage	`refers to the parent element's` `font size`
Netscape & IE	`implemented in both`

`<absolute>` values - any of the following:

```
xx-small|x-small|small|medium
   |large|x-large|xx-large

h1 { font-size:xx-large;} /* very large */
h2 {font-size:medium;}    /*   medium   */
h3 {font-size:xx-small;}  /* very small */
```

Exactly how these work depends on the table of font sizes computed and retained by the browser. Netscape and IE tend to display different sizes for the same value with Netscape tending to display larger than IE.

`<relative>` values
```
larger | smaller
```
These will become relative to the size of the parent element. It is probably safer to avoid using the relative and absolute values.

`<length>` values
Length-values comprise either absolute or relative *units* (not to be confused with the absolute and relative *values* given above. Ain't life grand?). We shall discuss them here in some detail so that you will know how they are used and interpreted by other properties which take *length* values. The following is taken from Section 4.3.2 of the W3C CSS2

Specification. The full document can be found at:
`http://www.w3.org/TR/REC-CSS2/`

Since readers have been advised to periodically visit the home site of W3C to keep abreast of developments in CSS, XHTML and XML, it may prove useful to let you read a portion of the document from which the following is taken. Details of the copyright notice are given in the Trademarks section of this text, together with the Status of the document from which the following is taken. Underlined text are links in the original electronic version to definitions used. The formatting is my own.

"There are two types of length units: relative and absolute.

Relative length units specify a length relative to another length property. Style sheets that use relative units will more easily scale from one medium to another (e.g., from a computer display to a laser printer).

Relative units are:
- **em**: the 'font-size' of the relevant font
- **ex**: the 'x-height' of the relevant font
- **px**: pixels, relative to the viewing device

Example(s):
```
H1 { margin: 0.5em }      /* em */
H1 { margin: 1ex }        /* ex */
P  { font-size: 12px }    /* px */
```

The 'em' unit is equal to the computed value of the 'font-size' property of the element on which it is used. The exception is when 'em' occurs in the value of the 'font-size' property itself, in which case it refers to the font size of the parent element. It may be used for vertical or horizontal measurement. (This unit is also sometimes called the quad-width in typographic texts.)
The 'ex' unit is defined by the font's 'x-height'. The x-height is so called because it is often equal to the height of the lowercase "x". However, an 'ex' is defined even for fonts that don't contain an "x".

Example(s):

The rule:
```
H1 { line-height: 1.2em }
```
means that the line height of H1 elements will be 20% greater than the font size of the H1 elements. On the other hand:
```
H1 { font-size: 1.2em }
```
means that the font-size of H1 elements will be 20% greater than the font size inherited by H1 elements.

.... extra information here, but is omitted ...

Absolute length units are only useful when the physical properties of the output medium are known. The absolute units are:

- **in**: inches -- 1 inch is equal to 2.54 centimeters.
- **cm**: centimeters
- **mm**: millimeters
- **pt**: points -- the points used by CSS2 are equal to 1/72th of an inch.
- **pc**: picas -- 1 pica is equal to 12 points.

Example(s):
```
H1 { margin: 0.5in }         /* inches  */
H2 { line-height: 3cm }      /* centimeters */
H3 { word-spacing: 4mm }     /* millimeters */
H4 { font-size: 12pt }       /* points */
H4 { font-size: 1pc }        /* picas */
```

In cases where the specified length cannot be supported, user agents must approximate it in the actual value."

<%> - Percentage - Values

There is a final type of value which is a percentage value. These are often the simplest way to specify font sizes. Such values are interpreted by the browser as being relative to the size of the parent element of the element you are describing. For example, if you specify the size of some bold text as being 120%, and the parent has a 10-point size, the bold text will be in 12-point, 120% of 10 being 12.

```
blockquote {font-size:10pt;} /* the parent */
strong     {font-size:120%;} /* the child  */
```

You should be careful about mixing different typefaces when setting font sizes. Each font family has preset character sizes. 12 points in one family will not necessarily be exactly the same size in another family.

`font` - (shorthand)

Some properties have a shorthand. For example:

```
p {font-family:"comic sans ms", sans-serif;
   font-size:12pt;
   font-variant:small-caps;
   font-weight:lighter;
   font-style:italic;}
```

could be written more simply as:

```
p {font:"comic sans ms", sans-serif  12pt
        small-caps lighter italic;}
```

Note how a *space* separates one set of property values from another in the shorthand syntax except for the two possible values for `font-family` where a *comma* has to be used. The values may be given in any order, the reason being that one property value can only be associated with one particular property. Thus, `italic` can be associated only with `font-style`, `sans-serif` only with `font-family`, and so on. Those values which are not mentioned take their default initial value as laid out in the browser's default style sheet.

CSS2 have included the `font-stretch` and the `font-size-adjust` properties. They do not work in Netscape 4 or IE5. See the W3C CSS2 Specification for details.

Here is an example using some of the font properties. It is a poor example of typography, but we shall be able to improve its appearance using some of the other properties covered in the next few chapters.

136

USING SOME FONT PROPERTIES

We are going to use some of the font properties in this section.

This is an important piece of text, so it is coloured red and set to 16 points.
This is a normal piece of text, so it will inherit the properties set by the User Agent for the body element.
This is some text with low priority, so it is coloured teal and set to 9 points.

```
<?xml version="1.0" encoding="UTF-8"?>
<!DOCTYPE html
     PUBLIC "-//W3C//DTD XHTML 1.0
     Transitional//EN"
     http://www.w3.org/TR/xhtml1/DTD/
     xhtml1-transitional.dtd">
<html xmlns="http://www.w3.org/1999/xhtml"
     xml:lang="en" lang="en">
<head>
<title>Using Font Properties Exercise</title>
<style>
h2 {font-size:x-large;
    font-family:"comic sans ms", sans-serif;
    font-variant:small-caps;}
div.important {color:red;
    background-color:transparent;
    font: 16pt serif;}
div.low {color:teal;
    background-color:transparent;
    font-size:9pt;}  </style> </head>
```

```
<body>
<h2>Using Some Font Properties</h2>
<p>We are going to use some of the font
properties in this section.</p>
<div class="important">
This is an important piece of text, so it is
coloured red and set to 16 points.</div>
<div>
This is a normal piece of text, so it will
inherit the properties set by the User Agent
for the body element.</div>
<div class="low">
This is some text with low priority, so it is
coloured teal and set to 9 points.</div>
</body>
</html>
```

Notes:

1. Since we have not given a style rule for the `p` selector, it will inherit its properties from its parent, which, as the source code stands, is `<body>`.

2. We have included the generic `sans-serif` value to stop the W3C Validator, quite rightly, from giving us a warning message. Likewise, we have included the `background-color` property. The W3C Validator does not like to see the `color` property used without an accompanying `background-color` property.

3. What I have discovered, simply by trial and error, is that the font *shorthand* (used with the `div.important` class selector) requires more than one value, otherwise it is treated as an error. If you have two values, then the Validator likes the first to refer to the font-size value. If you have three or more, any old order seems to satisfy the Validator.

I have not seen any explicit reference to the above in the Specification or elsewhere. But, perhaps, I may have missed something somewhere along the line.

What you have learnt

We have looked at basic syntax of style rules and listed the various categories for style properties. The `font` properties have been discussed in detail.

We saw that the parent-child inheritance is important when applying style rules and saw how to display the family tree by saving our XHTML document with an `.xml` extension and opening it in IE5.

The *length* and *percentage* values were discussed when we examined the font-size property. Finally we saw how to use the `font` shorthand property.

Test

1. Why will the W3C Validator give warning messages for the following style rules?

```
p {color:red;}
body {font-family:arial,helvetica;}
```

2. Who are the parents and who are the children of the elements used in the following extract?

```
<body>
<div> <p>some text <b>in bold</b> </p>
</div>
</body>
```

3. How can you get IE5 to show you the family tree for one of your XHTML documents?

4. What do the following length values mean?

```
12pt   12px   12pc
```

5. How many errors can you find in the following?

```
<style>
h2 {font-style:small caps;
font-size:12pts;text-colour:"teal': }
</style>
```

6. a) What font size will each of the paragraphs have, given the following source code?

```
<style type="text/css">
p {font-size: 20pt; color:red;}
</style>
</head>
<body>
<p style="font-size:12pt">
First paragraph. </p>
<p> Second paragraph. </p>
```

b) What will be the text colour contained in the first and the second paragraphs?

7. What is wrong with this?

```
body {font:"comic sans ms", sans-serif, 12pt,
    red;}
```

12: Text & Color Properties

In this Chapter we shall look at text and color properties to see how we can improve the rather bland looking examples of the previous chapters.

Text Properties

`text-indent`

This property specifies the indentation of a first line of text in a block.

text-indent	
Value	`<length>|<%>|inherit`
Initial	`0`
Applies to:	`block elements`
Inherited	`yes`
Percentage	`refers to width of containing box`
Netscape & IE	`implemented in both`

Value

<length>	as described on page 133.
<%>	note that the indentation is a percentage of the width of the *containing box*
inherit	new to CSS2

The value of text-indent may be a *negative* value. This will allow for outdenting a heading, for example:

> ## Outdented Heading
> Note the outdented heading. This paragraph has a first line indent and has been brought closer to the heading via the margin-top property. See Chapter 14.

```
<head>
<title>a frame document with css2</title>
<style type="text/css">
body {margin-left:2em; }
h2   {font-size:14pt; color:black;
     text-indent:-10pt; }
p     {text-indent:1em; margin-top:-12pt;}
</style>
</head>
<body>
<h2>Outdented Heading</h2>
<p>Note the outdented heading. This paragraph
has a first line indent and has been brought
closer to the heading via the margin-top
property. See Chapter 14.</p>
</body> </html>
```

Note: When outdenting, we frequently need to set margins for the body selector, otherwise the outdented text is cut off at the left margin. See Chapter 14 for the use of the margin properties.

Blocks revisited

We often need to make a distinction between block and inline elements when these are used as CSS selectors, so that we can apply property features appropriately. For example, the text-indent property indents the first line of a block text element. Therefore, suitable elements would be <p>, <div>, <blockquote> but not <i>, <form>, <img> or <span>.

In the following, the <body> element is the master block containing all the other block and inline elements.

```
<body>
Here is some text.
<p> More text in a <b>paragraph</b>
element.</p>
A third piece of text.
</body>
```

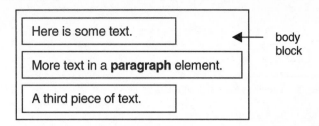

Here is some text.

More text in a **paragraph** element.

A third piece of text.

body block

The entire display is contained within the body block. This contains one paragraph block and two stray lines of text. But because the paragraph has its own block, the two other pieces of text ('Here is some text.' and 'A third piece of text.') have to be in blocks outside of the middle block. These two are called *anonymous* blocks in W3C parlance. So, we have four blocks in total.

Having stray lines of text is not good practice when using CSS, as the example on the next page illustrates. In the above example, suppose we want the `<p>` block and the two anonymous blocks to be indented. We could specify a text indent for the `body` selector. This will work in IE but, annoyingly, not fully in Netscape. To ensure that both main browsers do exactly as I want, I would be inclined to use three division or paragraph elements and apply the `text-indent` property to that selector. If one of the divisions required some special treatment, then a class attribute could be added.

Initial 0 value for text-indent
0 is the initial value. It is a length value and there will be no indentation. The zero length is unique in that it does not need to take a unit identifier (pt, em, cm, etc.).

Inherited
This states whether the property can be inherited from a parent. Thus, in the following source code, the `div` selector is text-indented by 0.5em. Any `<p>` child of `<div>` will also be indented but by an additional indent. Unfortunately, IE and Netscape handle block elements in different ways.

```
<style type= "text/css">
  div.indent {text-indent:0.5em;}
</style>
</head>
<body>
<p>A normal paragraph which is not indented.
</p>
<div class="indent">
Here is some text within the DIV block.
<p>This P text will inherit the text-indent
from its parent DIV.INDENT.</p>
A third line also indented because it is part
of the DIV.INDENT block.
</div>
<p>Another paragraph which is not indented
because it is not a child of DIV.INDENT. </p>
</body>
</html>
```

In the above, Netscape seems to treat the entire `div` as a single block and does not indent any children within the `div` element. In other words, the first line of the division is the only line to become indented. (Ah! Such is life.) Here is what IE5 will do.

A normal paragraph which is not indented.

Here is some text within the DIV block.

This P text will inherit the text-indent from its parent DIV.INDENT.

A third line also indented because it is part of the DIV.INDENT block.

Another paragraph which is not indented because it is not a child of DIV.INDENT.

The first and last `<p>` block will not be indented. The two anonymous blocks and the `<p>` block within the `<div>` tag are indented. But, notice that the `<p>` block is given an additional indent.

`text-align`

This property sets the horizontal justification of its element.

text-align	
Value	`left|center|right|justify|inherit`
Initial	`UA specific`
Applies to:	`block elements`
Inherited	`yes`
Percentage	`not available`
Netscape & IE	`implemented in both`

Clearly, this property cannot be applied to inline elements such as `<b>` or `<em>`, but can be applied to block level elements such as `<p>` `<div>` and `<body>`.

Example:

`div {text-align:justify;}`

Note that the `justify` value applies full right-left justification.

`text-decoration`

This property controls the decorative effects of text contained in elements.

text-decoration	
Value	`none|underline|overline|blink|` `line-through|inherit`
Initial	`none`
Applies to:	`all elements`
Inherited	`no`
Percentage	`not available`
Netscape & IE	`implemented in both except` `overline in Netscape.`

- The `overline` is an interesting value.
- All UAs must support the `blink` value but are free to ignore it. It is a naff thing to do anyway.
- By using the `none` value, we can prevent hypertext links from being underlined, something many of us have wanted to do for a long time.

145

```
<style type="text/css">
a:link     {text-decoration:none;}
a:visited {text-decoration:none;}
a:active   {text-decoration:none;}
</style>
```

What is the colon doing after the letter 'a'? It indicates a *pseudo-class*.

Pseudo-Classes

In CSS, most elements can be given style properties based on their position in the *document tree* but not all. The anchor element is one of these. Pseudo-classes were introduced to overcome the problem. The CSS2 Specification goes into this in more detail for those of you who would like to know more, especially Web Managers.

A class, as we have seen, is written like this:

`selector.classname {font-size:200%;}`

To distinguish the special pseudo-classes, a different syntax is used and the class name has also been reserved.

`selector:pseudo-classname {color:red;}`

a:link   refers to a hypertext link which has not yet been visited.

a:visited refers to an anchor element which has been visited.

a:active refers to a link which has been clicked but the resource has not yet been displayed.

None of the above can be put in the *document tree* because the tree is constructed once, when the page is first loaded. However, we may wish to choose some style for them. Hence, the inclusion of these pseudo classes. *(Again, may I refer to the CSS2 Specification for more syntax and other pseudo classes, especially if you are a Web Manager and are also interested in the Web as a printed medium.)*

Because the three reserved pseudo-class names can refer only to the anchor element, the following is valid since they imply the a selector.

```
:link {text-decoration:none;
       color:fuchsia; font-weight:bold;}
```

Likewise, we can do the following:

```
:link, :visited, :active
                {text-decoration:none;}
```

When multiple selectors take the same declarations, they can be separated by commas. In the following, all heading levels 1-3 would be in Arial:

```
h1,h2,h3 {font-family:arial, sans-serif;}
```

CSS2 also allows the following - *but do note the absence of the colon this time!*

```
a[href] {text-decoration:none; color:maroon;}
```

Here, the style is applied to any <a> element with the attribute href, no matter what value it has, active, visited or link. So any of the above can be used in place of the original long-winded method. You will begin to see these alternative forms of syntax as CSS becomes more widely used. So it is important to meet them now.

Be careful with the overline value when using anchor elements. You may end up with an overline *and* an underline. The overline does not suppress the underline in IE5.

text-transform
This property controls the capitalisation of an element's contained text. But note the US spelling for *capitalize*.

text-transform	
Value	capitalize|uppercase |lowercase|none|inherit
Initial	none
Applies to:	all elements

Inherited	yes
Percentage	not available
Netscape & IE	implemented in both

capitalize: puts the first character of each word into capitals
uppercase: all characters of each word are in uppercase
lowercase: all characters of each word are in lowercase
none: no effect. The author's case is preserved.

The actual transformation is typeface dependent. Some typefaces have no lowercase, e.g. Beesknees ITC.

`h1 {text-transform:uppercase;}`

`vertical-align`

This property affects the vertical positioning of the element itself within its *line box*. Suppose a paragraph has three lines. Each line would have a line height and its own line box.

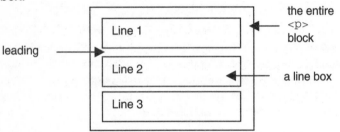

vertical-align	
Value	baseline|sub|super|top|text-top |middle | bottom | text-bottom <%> | <length>
Initial	baseline
Applies to:	inline elements
Inherited	no
Percentage	refers to line height of the element itself
Netscape & IE	not implemented in either except for super and sub in IE5

baseline: this is the bottom line upon which the characters rest. However, each line has *leading* (pronounced *ledding*) to separate lines of text. In the print industry of the past, printers put in thin strips of the metal lead to separate lines of text so that we could read the characters more easily. Without some form of leading, the lines of text would be difficult to read.

Consequently, a line of text with a font size of, say, point size 12, has some space added between the lines. By default, most browsers add 10% for the leading, resulting in a line height of 13.2pt. The line height (the font text plus the leading) is measured from the baseline of one line to the baseline of the next line. What this means is that half the leading (actually known as *half-leading*) is placed before the text and the other half after it. Thus, if you set a line of text at 12pt with a line height of 14pt, 2 points go before the text and 2 points after it. As we shall see with the next property, `line-height`, we can add our own spacing (*leading*) between lines of text.

sub & super: these lower or raise, respectively, the baseline of the parent's box for subscripts and superscripts. However, it does not affect the font size, so the `font-size` property will also be required if the text is to be made smaller, as in H_2O.

```
span { color:red; vertical-align:sub;
       font-size:8pt; }
```

Apart from the `sub` and `super`, the others are not implemented as yet. See the CSS2 Specification for details so that when browsers implement these features you will know what they can do.

Here are three properties which can create some highly desirable effects: `line-height`, `word-spacing` and `letter-spacing`.

line-height
This property allows the author to specify the distance or *leading* between lines, effectively giving us that feature

possessed by word processors for single, one-and-a-half or double line spacing.

line-height	
Value	`normal|<#>|<length>|<%>|inherit`
Initial	`normal`
Applies to:	`all elements`
Inherited	`yes`
Percentage	`refers to the font size of the element itself`
Netscape & IE	`implemented in both`

normal: the user agent (browser) computes a reasonable value. The CSS2 recommendation is between the number 1.0 and 1.2.

<#>: this is the number value which acts as a multiplication factor. Negative values are illegal.

<length>: the box height is set in em, pt, pc, etc., as defined on page 134. Negative values are illegal.

<%>: the percentage multiplied by the element's font size.

The following three examples result in the same line height.

```
div {font-size:10pt; line-height:1.2;}      number
div {font-size:10pt; line-height:1.2em;}     length
div {font-size:10pt; line-height:120%;}        %
```

word-spacing
This sets the spacing between words.

word-spacing	
Value	`normal|<length>|inherit`
Initial	`normal`
Applies to:	`all elements`
Inherited	`yes`
Percentage	`not available`
Netscape & IE	`not implemented in either`

normal: The normal inter-word spacing as defined by the current font and/or browser.

<length>: Gives the inter-word spacing *in addition to* the normal default spacing. Values may be negative but there may be implementation limits.

Example:

```
h1 {word-spacing:1em;}
```

em value

Em Space: A distance equal to the type size - 12 points in a 12 point typeface; 11 points in an 11 point typeface, and so on. Also known as a *mutton*.

Emdash: A dash the width of the letter "m" used in text to separate a parenthetical note as an alternate to parenthesis.

En space: Half an em. Also known as a *nut*.

The above definitions were taken from the following web site, a place which you may wish to visit, especially the section on Typography Glossary.

```
http://www.redsun.com/type/
```

You have to be careful when using certain types of values. Some directly influence the element itself, others by what the element *inherits*. Using a length value `em`, consider the following:

```
p {line-height: 1.2em;}
```

means that the line height of `p` elements will be 20% greater than the font size of the `p` elements. On the other hand:

```
h1 {font-size: 1.2em;}
```

means that the font-size of `h1` elements will be 20% greater than the font size *inherited* by `h1` elements.

```
letter-spacing
```

This allows spacing between letters and the values are the same as for word spacing.

letter-spacing	
Value	`normal|<length>|inherit`
Initial	`normal`

Applies to:	all elements
Inherited	yes
Percentage	not available
Netscape & IE	not implemented in Netscape 4

There are two more properties in CSS2 which you may wish to look up in the W3C Specification. Neither work in IE5 or Netscape 4, but one day ......! They are the `text-shadow` and `white-space` properties.

We shall look at the `color` property now, and then you can apply some of the properties covered in this chapter to your own examples.

color

This property sets the colour of an element's text.

color	
Value	<color>|inherit
Initial	depends on browser, usually black
Applies to:	all elements
Inherited	yes
Percentage	not available
Netscape & IE	implemented in both

<color>:

A color is selected in one of three ways in CSS:

- using one of the 16 keyword colour names
- using the hexadecimal numbers for RGB (red, green, blue)
- using the rgb(n,n,n) function

Colour Names

There are sixteen common colour names which most browsers can recognise.

Colour name	Hex value	Colour name	Hex value
black	"#000000"	green	"#00FF00"
silver	"#C0C0C0"	lime	"#008000"
gray (US spelling)	"#808080"	olive	"#808080"

152

white	"#FFFFFF"	yellow	"#FFFF00"
maroon	"#800000"	navy	"#000080"
red	"#FF0000"	blue	"#0000FF"
purple	"#800080"	teal	"#008080"
fuchsia	"#FF00FF"	aqua	"#00FFFF"

Using hexadecimal numbers

If a colour name is not used, then we need to use either its hexadecimal number or the `rgb()` function. Both methods use three sets of numbers each specifying red, green and blue (RGB) in that order. These are the three colours used by TV and PC monitors. PCs have 256 variations from 0 - 255 for each colour. When using hexadecimal numbers, each of the three colours takes a pair of hex numbers resulting in six numbers with no spaces and leading zeroes. FF is the hexadecimal number for 255, the purest value for each colour. Mixing the three pure colours of red, green and blue results in pure white. (Monitors are governed by the laws of Physics.) Thus: `color="#ffffff"` is pure white and `color="#000000"` is pure black. Every variation in between gives all the colours and shades of grey which a monitor can display.

Hexadecimal

The hexadecimal number system has sixteen digits: 0-15, whereas our decimal system has ten: 0-9 and the binary system only two: 0-1. All number systems include zero, hence 0-15 for the sixteen hexadecimal digits.

In hexadecimal, the digits 10 - 15 are given letters:

A=10, B=11, C=12, D=13, E=14, F=15.

Thus, D in hexadecimal is the equivalent of the decimal number 13.

A two-digit hex number is sufficient for the 256 variations for each colour. 00 - FF is the range 0 - 255 in decimal. Thus each displayed colour has a six-digit hex code.

Colour	Hex code RRGGBB
pure red	FF0000
pure green	00FF00
pure blue	0000FF
dark blue	090DEE

The following style rules would colour paragraph text thus:

```
p {color=#FF0000;} paragraph text in red
p {color=#00ff00;} paragraph text in green
p {color=#00F;}    paragraph in blue
```

The value of the color property should be preceded by a hash symbol (#) with no spaces. Case is not significant.

With style sheets, a shorter version may be used when both hex numbers are the same. Thus `#334455` could be written as `#345`. Note that XHTML does not support this shorthand, in other words the following:

```
<font color="#345">some text </font>
```

would be invalid.

How to work out the hex number for any colour

In Windows, it is very simple to discover the hexadecimal numbers for a particular colour. Use any application which permits you to create your own colours with the *Custom* tab of the colour palette. For example, in Word, Excel or PowerPoint, simply draw a rectangle or circle using the appropriate drawing toolbar shape. Then, use the down arrow on the '*Fill Color*' icon and choose '*More Fill Colors*' and then the *Custom* tab.

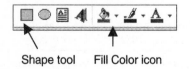

Shape tool   Fill Color icon

When you choose your colour, you will see the decimal numbers for the RGB in decimal.

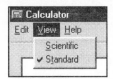

Simply convert the decimal numbers into hexadecimal. This is easy in the *scientific* view of Windows *Calculator*. Type in the decimal number and click the Hex box. The decimal number will be converted to a hexadecimal number - 7B below. These can then be used as the value for the color property.

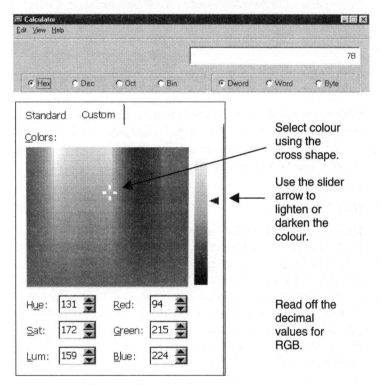

Select colour using the cross shape.

Use the slider arrow to lighten or darken the colour.

Read off the decimal values for RGB.

Tip for those grey days:
If you subtract equal amounts from RGB you get shades of grey. Thus: `aaaaaa,` `bbbbbb,` *etc.*

or: `111111,` `222222,` *etc.*

or even: `e1e1e1,` `a5a5a5,` *etc.*

But 556677 *is not equal amounts and thus a colour results!*

Using the `rgb(rn,gn,bn)` colour function

This is not supported in XHTML, only in CSS. If you do not wish to convert numbers to hexadecimal, they can be left in decimal and used as follows. Taking the decimal values shown in the above illustration, we could write:

```
p {color:rgb(94,215,224);}
```

We shall cover just one of the background properties here and deal with the rest in the next Chapter. The reason for covering it here, is that if you validate your style sheet via the W3C Validator and do not include a `background-color` property each time you use the `color` property, it gives you a warning message.

`background-color`

This property sets the background colour of an element. Do not mistake it for the `color` property which sets the colour of the text, known as the *foreground colour*.

background-color	
Value	`<color>|transparent|inherit`
Initial	`transparent`
Applies to:	`all elements`
Inherited	`no`
Percentage	`not available`
Netscape & IE	`implemented in both`

<color>: takes the values as mentioned for the color property on page 152.

transparent: this will allow the colour of the parent's *box* colour to shine through. We discuss the meaning of *box* in Chapter 14. For the present, this value permits the parent-element's colour to act as the background. Typically, this will be whatever colour has been set in the `<body>` element. White is often the default.

156

```
body {color:red; background-color:silver;}
p    {font-size:12pt; color:teal;
      background-color:transparent;}
```

The above sets all text to red and the background colour to silver. However, because we have included a style rule for all paragraph text, this rule will set all such text to teal with a transparent background. Consequently, the text will have a silver background colour. But if we change the style rule to:

```
p {font-size:12pt; color:teal;
   background-color:rgb(255,0,0);}
```

the text boxes will have a red background. Not a pretty sight but it illustrates how the properties work.

> *Tip:* To satisfy the W3C CSS Validator, a background-color property must be used when a color property is set. Consequently, use the background-color set to transparent to prevent warning messages appearing when you do not want to set a specific background colour.

IE and Netscape behave differently by how much background is actually coloured. IE tends to colour up to the right margin, whereas Netscape colours up to the last character resulting in a 'box' with a ragged right justification.

Note how much of this paragraph text is actually coloured when viewed in Internet Explorer. Note how it is boxed at the right.

Note how much of this paragraph text is actually coloured when viewed in Netscape. Note the ragged right.

What you have learnt

We have looked at the text and color properties. We have learnt how important it is to know whether an element is a block or inline element since this affects which properties we can apply to selectors.

The inheritance of properties plays a major role with some of the elements.

We also learnt about *pseudo-classes* for the anchor selector and how we can prevent hyperlinks being underlined. We also discussed the three ways of setting values for the `color` property in CSS.

The line-height, letter spacing and color properties should make our web pages more pleasing.

13: Background Properties

`background-image`

This property allows you to set an image as a background rather than a colour.

background-image	
Value	`uri│none│inherit`
Initial	`none`
Applies to:	`all elements`
Inherited	`no`
Percentage	`not available`
Netscape & IE	`implemented in both`

uri: this is the new way of referring to a URL (Uniform Resource Locator). It includes a URN and a URL, thus:
URN + URL = URI. (Uniform Resource Identifier)

> *So what is a URN? "An expected new way of identifying resources is called URN (Uniform Resource Name)." (sic W3C Specification.) So we shall have to wait to see how and where a URN can be used.*

Example:
```
body {background-image:url("some.gif");}
div  {background-image:none;}
```

Here, `some.gif` would be tiled throughout the body background, namely, the entire document window. Since the `<div>` has no image and by default it has a transparent background, the body's background image, `some.gif`, will appear as the division's background with any text in the `<div>` block superimposed on that image.

If we add a paragraph block with its own background image, that image will be tiled behind the paragraph text, blotting out the body's image.

```
p {background-image:url("some-other.gif");}
```

Note the syntax. The `url()` function encloses the image reference in round brackets. The quotes around the partial or complete URL are optional.

`background-repeat`

This is a very useful property. It permits an author to repeat an image vertically or horizontally or with just one single copy. Without this property, images are tiled horizontally and vertically throughout an element's block.

background-repeat	
Value	repeat│repeat-x│repeat-y │no-repeat│inherit
Initial	repeat
Applies to:	all elements
Inherited	no
Percentage	not available
Netscape & IE	implemented in both

repeat: this tiles an image both horizontally and vertically.
repeat-x: this will repeat an image only on the x-axis, i.e. horizontally.
repeat-y: this will repeat an image only on the y-axis, i.e. vertically.
no-repeat: the image is not repeated and only one copy will be seen.

Example:
```
body {background-image:url("some.gif");
      background-repeat:repeat-x;}
```

This would repeat the image across the width of the screen. But where will it be placed? At the top, just one tiled horizontal occurrence of the image. The vertical equivalent is placed down the far left. If `no-repeat` is used, then the image appears once at the top-left of the screen. However, with the next property, we can decide on the exact position of the image.

`background-position`

If a background image has been specified, this property selects the initial position of the image.

background-position	
Value	`<%>│<length>│top│center│bottom │left│right│inherit`
Initial	`0% 0% - the x,y co-ordinates`
Applies to:	`block level elements`
Inherited	`no`
Percentage	`refers to the size of the box`
Netscape & IE	`not implemented in Netscape; IE has some limitations`

<%>: This takes a single or a pair of % values. If two are given, they specify the x-y co-ordinates, in other words the first value sets the position across the block, the second sets the down position. So 14% 50% would place the top-left corner of the image 14% across the box and 50% down. 0% 0% would place the top left corner of the image in the padding area's upper left corner. 100% 100% places the lower right corner of the image in the lower right corner of the block.

If a single value is given, it sets the horizontal position with the vertical always at 50%. When two values are given, the first must refer to the horizontal position.

<length>: Same as <%> but length units may be used. Thus: 2cm 3cm would place the top-left of the image 2cm across and 3cm down. IE5 does not recognise the second positioning in a `body` selector

top left or left top: same as 0% 0%
top or top center or center top: same as 50% 0%
right top or top right: same as 100% 0%

and so on for the other variations:

`bottom right/left/center.`

There are so many variations with the positioning that it is not possible to say which work and which do not. In general, Netscape does not recognise this property. IE5 is limited especially with the second percentage and length values. You will have to test them out.

`background-attachment`

This property allows a background image to be fixed or scrolled. If it is fixed, it stays in the same position, even when the user scrolls the page, rather like clouds scudding across a fixed moon. With the right sort of image, you could create a watermark which stays fixed even when the rest of the document is scrolled.

background-attachment	
Value	`scroll|fixed|inherit`
Initial	`scroll`
Applies to:	`all elements`
Inherited	`no`
Percentage	`not available`
Netscape & IE	`not implemented in Netscape`

fixed: this is the one to use to fix your background image. The `scroll` simply moves the image in the normal way. The `fixed` value has little impact unless used with the `body` element.

Example:

```
<style type="text/css">
body {color:red; background-color:pink;
    background-image:url("back.gif");
    background-repeat:no-repeat;
    background-position: 2cm 1cm;
    background-attachment:fixed;}
</style>
```

This would set the image 2 cm from the left and 1 cm down the screen. It would appear once (no-repeat) and would remain fixed even when the reader scrolls the rest of the document. It can be very effective.

`background` - (shorthand)

This is a shorthand way of writing values for some or all of the background properties. It first sets all the individual

162

background properties to their initial values and then assigns any explicit values given in the declaration. Thus, any property value not mentioned takes on its initial value.

background	
Value	`background-color`| `background-image`| `background-repeat`| `background-attachment`| `background-position`|`inherit`
Initial	`there can be no single initial` `value when using shorthands`
Applies to:	`all elements`
Inherited	`no`
Percentage	`available for position only`
Netscape & IE	`Netscape selects those properties` `it has implemented`

Examples:

`body { background: red; }`

Only a value for the `background-color` has been given. All other individual properties are given their initial values.

`p {background: gray url("animage.png") repeat`
`                fixed 50% }`

In the second declaration, all individual properties have been specified. The values may be given in any order.

What you have learnt

We have seen how to use images as backgrounds to our web pages. They can be placed anywhere we choose and even remain in a fixed position whilst the rest of the document scrolls. This can be very effective for the right sort of web page.

14: Margin, Border & Padding Properties

Before we can discuss the `margin`, `border` and `padding` properties, we need to understand how browsers create the boxes which are generated for block elements. Block elements are closely related to their boxes.

The Box Model

Every block element lives in its own box along with any of its inline elements. So the `<p>`, `<body>`, `<blockquote>`, `<ul>`, etc., each have their space or box. Inside this box is the content, such as an image or text.

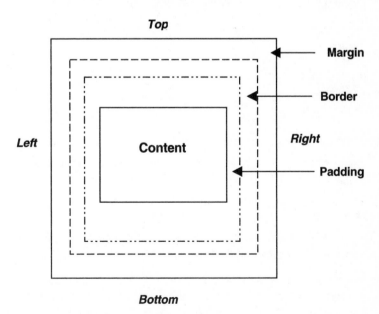

Each box has an optional `margin`, `border` and `padding` property. When using these properties, we need to understand how they relate to each other. It is basic common sense, but the relationship and terminology in use has been defined by the W3C.

Margins, borders and padding each have a top, right, bottom and left. This is the order in which their values *must be* referred to when using the shorthand `margin` property.

> *Tip: I tend to think of the word TROUBLE with the vowels removed - TRBL - when I need to remember this order.*

Margin properties

These set the four margins and is an ideal way of creating whitespace margins without having to resort to HTML tables. The use of whitespace margins and line spacing via the `line-height` property can give a web page a pleasing layout, see the example on page 279 (Example 1).

margin-top, margin-right, margin-bottom, margin-left	
Value	`<length>|<%>|auto|inherit`
Initial	`0`
Applies to:	`all elements`
Inherited	`no`
Percentage	`refers to width of containing block`
Netscape & IE	`implemented in both`

<length>: specify a fixed width using the length values (see page 133)

<%>: when using percentages, the width is calculated with respect to the width of the *containing block*

auto: the default width used by the browser, usually the same as the zero length value

Negative values are also allowed so that a heading, for example, could be outdented. When using negative values for margins, it is advisable to give the body block an appropriate margin to prevent an inner block with a negative margin 'disappearing' off the screen. Thus:

```
body {margin-left:1cm;}
h1   {margin-left:-0.5cm;}
```

Now the heading has some screen space to move into.

Here is an example of creating whitespace using the margin property and the line-height property.

```
body {margin-left:2cm; margin-right:2cm;
      font-size:10pt; line-height:15pt;}
```

The content of the entire page has a left and right margin of 2 centimetres. The text has a font size of 10 points with line spacing of one-and-a-half.

The Containing Block

This is the box which is generated via a block element, and which may contain other boxes generated by its child block elements. Thus, the `<body>` element is the containing box for all boxes generated by other block elements such as `<div>`, `<table>`, `<ul>`, etc. A `<div>` block could be the containing box for other block elements, such `<p>`.

`margin` **(shorthand)**

margin (shorthand)	
Value [1 - 4]	`<length>`I`<%>`Iauto Iinherit
Initial	`not defined for shorthands`
Applies to:	`all elements`
Inherited	`no`
Percentage	`refers to width of containing block`
Netscape & IE	`mainly implemented in both`

Value [1 - 4]: This abbreviation, used in the W3C reference, means that there must be at least *one* value and a *maximum* of 4 values.

If *one* value is given, it applies to all four margins TRBL (top, right, bottom, left).

If *two* values are given, the first applies to the top and bottom, the second to the right and left.

If *three* values are given, the first refers to the top, the second to the right *and* left, the third to the bottom. Watch out for this.

If *four* values are given, each applies to the standard order of top, right, bottom and left (TRBL).

Examples:

```
div {margin:0.5in;}
```

the content of the division will have a margin of 0.5 inches for all four edges.

```
div {margin:0.5in 0.3in;}
```

the top and bottom will have a 0.5in margin, the right and left a 0.3in margin.

```
div {margin:0.5in 0.4in 0.3in;}
```

the top margin is set to 0.5in; the right and left to 0.4in, and the bottom to 0.3in.

```
h1 {margin-left:2cm; margin-bottom:0;}
p {margin-top:0; margin-left:2.2cm;}
```

This will effectively cause a heading to be indented by 2cm, and any contained paragraphs to be indented by 2.2cm, with the vertical space between the heading and the first paragraph to close up due to the margin-bottom of the heading being set to zero and the margin-top of the paragraph being set to zero. (This does not work in Netscape.)

```
body {margin-top:1cm; margin-left:2cm;}
```

The content of the body element will be pushed 1 centimetre down at the top, and 2cm to the left. The bottom and right will be set to zero and to whatever distance from the right the browser usually makes for window content.

The following shows how you can close the gap between horizontal rules and headings.

```
<style type="text/css">
h3 { margin-top:0in; margin-bottom:0in;}
</style>
```

Without Margin Properties

With Margin Properties

Here is how we can close the gap between a heading and a following paragraph text, but it is not supported in Netscape.

```
<style type="text/css">
h1 {margin-bottom: 0;
    margin-left: 1cm;}
p {margin-top:0; margin-left:1.3cm;}
</style>
</head>
<body>
<h1>Margin Heading in Internet Explorer</h1>
<p> Some text follows here ...</p>
... etc. ...
</body>
```

Margin Heading in Internet Explorer
Some text follows here ...

Margin Heading in Netscape 4

Some text follows here ...

With the above properties, you can now precisely position your headings and text blocks within the screen. Each heading level could be given its own indent space.

Be Aware of the following:

1. Margins are always transparent so the background colour of the containing box will always shine through.

2. Margins can be given negative values, so that text can be made to overlap should this be desirable. Netscape does support negative margins.

```
h1 {text-transform: capitalize;
    margin-bottom: 0;
    margin-left: 1cm;}
p {margin-top:-0.3cm; margin-left:1.3cm;}
```

3. When margins adjoin, the following rules apply. Horizontal margins are not collapsed. Vertical margins are collapsed and the larger margin will be used.

padding properties

These properties define the padding width of a box. Unlike the margin properties, values for padding values *cannot be negative*. Like the margin properties, percentage values for padding properties refer to the width of the generated box's containing block. The values are the same as those for margins with the exception of negative values.

padding-top, padding-right, padding-bottom, padding-left	
Value	`<length>|<%>|auto|inherit`
Initial	`0`
Applies to:	`all elements`
Inherited	`no`
Percentage	`refers to width of containing block`
Netscape & IE	`implemented in both`

170

Example: `blockquote {padding-top:0.3em;}`

`padding` (shorthand)

padding (shorthand)	
Value [1 - 4]	`<length>|<%>|auto|inherit`
Initial	`not defined for shorthands`
Applies to:	`all elements`
Inherited	`no`
Percentage	`refers to width of containing block`
Netscape & IE	`implemented in both`

This behaves in a similar manner to the margin shorthand. When using margins and padding, you need to take *both* widths into account. It is worth experimenting with various widths to see their effect. That is how you will begin to see how they can be applied.

I find length values easier to use initially, since it is simpler to work out whether the desired effect has taken place.

```
<style type="text/css">
body {font-family:arial, sans-serif;}
h1 {font-size:12pt;
    margin-bottom: 0;
    margin-left: 1cm;}
p {margin-top:0; margin-left:1.3cm;}
</style>
</head>
<body>
<h1>Margin Heading in Internet Explorer</h1>
<p> The cow jumped over the moon, and the
little dog barked to see such fun and the cat
ran away with the spoon.</p>
```

Margin Heading in Internet Explorer

The cow jumped over the moon, and the little dog barked to see such fun and the cat ran away with the spoon.

We have set margins in the above, but now let us add some padding to the heading: `padding-left:1cm;`

> ## Margin Heading in Internet Explorer
>
> The cow jumped over the moon, and the little dog barked to see such fun and the cat ran away with the spoon.

The heading margin and the padding left have been *combined* to indent the heading even further. The paragraph block remains in the same position. Take care when combining margins, padding and borders.

Margins are transparent as we mentioned earlier. But what colour does the padding area take? It takes on the colour of the element's `background-color`. If we give the heading element a background colour, we shall see this colour in the padding area.

Be aware that Netscape and IE5 have different approaches as to the amount of heading which is actually coloured. See page 157. Try the following in both browsers to see what effect each one gives. There are so many possible variations with these properties that you are encouraged to experiment.

```
<style type="text/css">
body {font-family:arial, sans-serif;
      background:blue;}
h1   {text-transform:uppercase;
      font-size:12pt;
      font-family:arial, sans-serif;
      margin-bottom: 0;
      margin-left: 1cm;
      padding-left:1cm;
      background:red;}
```

border properties

Neither of the two main browsers have fully implemented the border properties. Be warned, it is all very frustrating! See the *tip* on page 180. Those which are implemented produce different effects. You will have to test them out to see which apply. In general, Netscape prefers the shorthand version. IE5 is not totally happy when top, right, bottom and left are specified but like Netscape seems happy with the shorthands.

There are so many of these properties that you will be relieved to know that there are many shorthands available. Borders can be given not only a width but also a colour and a style (dashes, lines, etc.). Consequently, we have the `border-top-width`, `border-top-color` and `border-top-style`; `border-left-width|color|style`;

and so on, for the right and the bottom - 12 in all.

Here is the `border-right-width` property. The same values hold for the other three, `border-left-width`, etc.

border-right-width	
Value	`<length>|thick|thin|medium` `|inherit`
Initial	`medium`
Applies to:	`all elements`
Inherited	`no`
Percentage	`not available`
Netscape & IE	`patchy in both`

The interpretation of thick, medium and thin is browser dependent. All you can guarantee is that thin is less than or equal to medium and medium is less than or equal to thick. In other words, all three could have the same thickness.

$$thin <= medium <= thick$$

<length> values cannot be negative.

Fortunately there is a `border-width` shorthand.

border-width (shorthand)	
Value [1-4]	`<length>|thick|thin|medium` `|inherit`
Initial	`medium`

173

Applies to:	all elements
Inherited	no
Percentage	not available
Netscape & IE	mainly implemented in both

Value [1-4] has the same meaning as for the `margin`
`shorthand` given on page 167.

`body {border-width:1cm 2cm;}`

Here we are setting the top and bottom border widths to
1cm, and the right and left to 2cm.

Try the following in both Netscape and IE5. You may like to
experiment with different `color` and `width` values.

```
<?xml version="1.0" encoding="UTF-8"?>
<!DOCTYPE html
PUBLIC "-//W3C//DTD XHTML 1.0
Transitional//EN"
"http://www.w3.org/TR/xhtml1/DTD/xhtml1-
transitional.dtd">
<html xmlns="http://www.w3.org/1999/xhtml"
xml:lang="en" lang="en">
<head>
<title>Margins exercise</title>
<style type="text/css">
body {font-family:arial, sans-serif;
      background:#f00;
      border-width:1cm 2cm;}
h1   {font-size:12pt;
      font-family:arial, sans-serif;
      margin-bottom: 0;
      margin-left: 1cm;
      padding-left:1cm;}
p    {margin-top:0; margin-left:1.3cm;}
</style>
</head>
<body>
<h1>Margin Heading in Internet Explorer</h1>
<p> The cow jumped over the moon, and the
little dog barked to see such fun and the cat
ran away with the spoon.</p> </body> </html>
```

This is a good example of why it is convenient to separate content from presentation. The body code is easy to read and the style sheet can be adjusted to try out different effects.

Notice how scroll bars have been added by IE5.

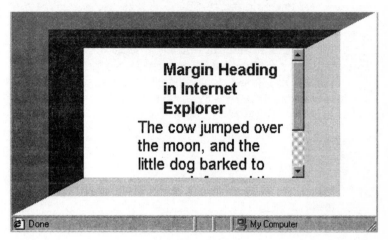

border-color properties

This property sets the colours for the four borders. We show the values for `border-right-color` which also apply to the other three sides. There is also a `border-color` shorthand.

border-right-color	
Value	`<color>|inherit`
Initial	`the value of the color property`
Applies to:	`all elements`
Inherited	`no`
Percentage	`not available`
Netscape & IE	`mainly implemented in both`

<color>: The values for `<color>` are the same as those described for the color property on page 152. We summarise them here for convenience. The color values may be any of the following:

175

- using one of the 16 keyword colour names
- using the hexadecimal numbers for RGB (red, green, blue)
- using the hexadecimal shorthand #345
- using the rgb(n,n,n) function

```
div { border-top-color: #f00;
      border-right-color: #ff0000;
      border-bottom-color: rgb(255,0,0);
      border-left-color: silver;}
```

The first three are identical and all request the colour red. The left border will be silver. However, Netscape 4 does not like these long-winded declarations. In general, it prefers the shorthands. So here is the `border-color` shorthand.

border-color (shorthand)	
Value [1-4]	`<color>|transparent|inherit`
Initial	`the value of the color property`
Applies to:	`all elements`
Inherited	`no`
Percentage	`not available`
Netscape & IE	`mainly implemented in both`

Like the other shorthands, there may be from 1 to 4 settings. (However, Netscape 4 seems to select just one of them and not necessarily the first one either! ☹)

<color>: specifies a colour as given for the individual properties.

transparent: This is a tricky one. In IE, a `border-color` set to `transparent` will take on the same colour as the text's `color` property.

```
p {margin-top:0.5cm; text-align:justify;
   color:red;
   background:silver;
   border-color: transparent;
   border-style:solid;}
```

Here, because the text colour is red and the paragraph's border-color is set to transparent, the border will be red. Without the transparent value, it would still be red because the initial value is the same as the `color` property. But Netscape tends to choose black when the `transparent` value is set on the shorthand below! If you want some consistency between the two main browsers, you will have to set the colour using the *shorthand* `border` property (discussed below). You will also have to set a `border style` otherwise border colours do not display. This is what we discuss next.

```
p {border: solid transparent;} // see page 179
```

`border-style` properties
This property sets the style for a border, solid line, dashes, groove, etc. Again, there are four sides as well as the border-style shorthand. Here are the specific values for `border-top-style` which also apply to `border-right-style`, `border-bottom-style` and `border-left-style`.

border-top-style	
Value	`none|hidden|dotted|dashed|solid |double|groove|ridge|inset |outset|inherit`
Initial	`none`
Applies to:	`all elements`
Inherited	`no`
Percentage	`not available`
Netscape & IE	`implemented partially in both`

Values:

none: no border. It is computed to the value zero.

hidden: same as none, except that when used in tables it resolves any conflicts.

dotted | dashed: borders are a series of dots or dashes.

solid | double: a solid single line or double line.

groove: border looks as though it was carved into the background.

177

ridge: border looks as though it were coming out of the background.

inset: the border makes the entire box look as though it were embedded in the background.

outset: the border makes the entire box look as though it were coming out of the background.

However, do not get too excited by all these. The W3C Specification adds that "user agents may interpret 'dotted', 'dashed', 'double', 'groove', 'ridge', 'inset' and 'outset' to be solid." (*sic*)

IE accepts: none, solid, double, groove, ridge, inset and outset with certain elements, including body.

Netscape seems to ignore the `border-style` in all elements except the body element. However, it seems to accept the `border` shorthand (see page 180).

The following does not work in Netscape:

`h1 {border-style:solid; border-color:red;}`

but it does accept:

`h1 {border:solid red;}`

("Don't ask !" Fortunately, IE accepts this shorthand.)

You need to experiment with all the possible variations in both `body` and other block elements to see their effect.

Be aware that no borders will be visible unless a border style is given. If you do want borders to be visible, you must always include a border style. (IE is more tolerant than Netscape. But it is safer to get into the habit of always including a border style.)

`border-style` **(shorthand)**

border-style (shorthand)	
Value [1-4]	none|hidden|dotted|dashed|solid |double|groove|ridge|inset |outset|inherit

Initial	none
Applies to:	all elements
Inherited	no
Percentage	not available
Netscape & IE	patchy in Netscape

The values behave the same as for the `margin` shorthand on page 167. Thus:

```
#abc {border-style:solid groove;}
```

will apply a solid line to the horizontal top and bottom borders, and a groove for the vertical right and left borders. Well, that is the theory. In practice some combinations work for both main browsers, other combinations for just one, other combinations with neither. Have fun!

Individual border shorthands

Each side of the border has its own shorthand for setting the width, colour and style. We show this for the border-bottom shorthand below, but the same applies to the other three sides.

border-bottom (shorthand)	
Value	width|style|<color>|inherit
Initial	see individual properties
Applies to:	all elements
Inherited	no
Percentage	not available
Netscape & IE	implemented in IE

Example:

```
h1 {border-bottom: thick solid red;}
```

This would set the bottom border to a thick width, solid line style and colour red. Omitted values are set to their initial values. Thus:

```
h1 {border-bottom: thick solid;}
```

because the colour value is missing, the bottom border will take on the `color` property of the `h1` element. If this

179

element has not been given a `color` property, it will inherit the `color` property of its parent.

`border` (shorthand)

This shorthand property will set a border's width, colour and style on all four sides without resorting to the four shorthands above. Netscape seems happier with this shorthand rather than with some of the individual border properties.

border (shorthand)	
Value	width|style|<color>|inherit
Initial	see individual properties
Applies to:	all elements
Inherited	no
Percentage	not available
Netscape & IE	mainly implemented in both

Have you noticed that the `[1-4]` abbreviation is missing? Unlike the margin and padding shorthand, this property cannot set *different* values for each of the four sides. Values given with the border property will apply to *all four* sides. If different values are required, then you must use one or more of the `border-top|right|bottom|left` properties. Consequently:

```
blockquote {border:solid red thin;}
```

will apply a thin red solid border to all *four* sides of the `blockquote` content.

> *Tip: The best way to deal with borders so that most of what you want will work for both IE5 and Netscape 4, is to use the border shorthand and apply the effects to all four sides.*

Take these two pieces of code. The first works just in IE5 but the second will work for both main browsers.

```
blockquote.one {border-color:teal;
                border-style:groove;
                border-left:double green;
                color:black;}
```

180

```
blockquote.two {border:teal groove;
                color:black;}
```

Neither will work properly, unless a style value is set, for example, `solid`.

The float property

Finally, let us examine the `float` property. This allows text to flow around an image or to flow text around text and text around tables.

float	
Value	`left|right|none|inherit`
Initial	`none`
Applies to:	`all elements except positioned elements (see Chapter 15)`
Inherited	`no`
Percentage	`not available`
Netscape & IE	`both`

left: the element is floated to the left and the content of any following element wraps around the right.

right: same as left, except that the element floats on the right with other content appearing on the left.

none: the element is not floated.

The floated element generates a box which is floated left or right, or not floated. It may be set for elements which generate boxes provided that these are not absolutely positioned (see Chapter 15).

```
<head><title>Politicians</title>
<style type="text/css">

p.left {float:left; width:275px;
        color:black;
        padding-left:30px; padding:1em;}
p       {color:black;}
img     {margin-right:30px;}
</style> </head>

<body>
```

```
<h3> A Politician Speaks </h3>
<p class="left">
<img src="biddy.gif" align="left">

"There has been a sea change in the way that
the Piple of this great country now see how
the matter under discussion has
</p>

<p>
progressed under this government. Despite what
we inherited from the previous government, I
now address Conference,  blah blah blah. ..."
</p>

</body>
</html>
```

A Politician Speaks

 "There has been a sea change in the way that the Piple of this great country now see how the matter under discussion has

progressed under this government. Despite what we inherited from the previous government, I now address Conference, blah blah blah. ..."

What you have learnt

We have seen how to use the margin, padding and border properties. The latter has not been implemented consistently in the two main browsers, but the border shorthand does work for both provided that you wish to apply the values to all four sides.

The float property can produce some imaginative web pages, and I am sure you will be far more creative than I have been.

Test

1. You are surprised by the amount a heading (or paragraph, blockquote) text is indented. What factors will you take into account to adjust the amount of indentation?

2. What style rules would you use to create the following. Note how the horizontal rules are close to the heading.

Margin Heading in Internet Explorer

Some text follows here ...

---

3. How would the browser window behave with each of the following?

```
div {width:300px;}
div {width:80%;}
```

4. For the following style sheet:

```
<style type="text/css">
body       {color:rgb(0,0,255);
            font-family:helvetica, sans-serif;
            font-size:14pt; line-height:16pt;}
div.indent {margin-left:2em; margin-top:2em;
            color:#f00;}
</style>
<body>
<h1>Welcome to my Home Page </h1>
<div>Some welcome text ... </div>
<div class="indent">A special note follows
here ... </div>
</body>
```

a) What colour will the `div.indent` text be in?
b) What colour will the `<div>` text be in?
c) What indentation will the `<div>` text have?

15: Positioning Properties

In this Chapter, we shall look at the following:

- position property
- z-index
- visibility
- display

One of the interesting features of CSS from a web design and layout point of view, is the `position` property which allows a box element to be positioned by the author anywhere on the Web screen, including overlapping. The example on the next page gives an indication of what can be done.

In the past, web authors used tables to make their pages look more attractive. But tables take time to be laid out on a screen. In CSS2, the positioning features provide for a more accurate placement of text and images as well as taking less time to display. You will be pleased to hear that both Netscape 4 and, in particular, IE5 have implemented many of the positioning features. All the examples given have been tested in IE5.

Positioning elements

We have seen that elements reside in boxes or blocks. Thus, a paragraph, an image or a division element has its own block or space or position on the web page. One of the neat features of CSS is that it is possible to position block elements anywhere on a page, not to be confused with a block element's margin settings.

When using the `position` property, we often have to use additional properties to set the required position, typically, the `top`, `right`, `bottom` and `left` properties. Let us take the following example and then discuss the code.

Figure 15.1

```
<head>
<title> Overlapping Text with CSS2</title>
<style type="text/css">
h3      {font-family:arial, sans-serif;
         font-size:20pt; }
#css    {font-size:34pt;
         position:absolute;
         top:80px; left:100px;
         color:black; }
#and    {font-size:44pt;
         position:absolute;
         top:95px; left:170px; color:gray; }
#xhtml  {font-size:24pt;
         position:absolute;
         top:135px; left:210px; color:black;}
address {position:absolute; top:200px; }
</style>
</head>

<body>
<h3>Learn</h3>
<div id="css">CSS</div>
<div id="and">&amp;</div>
<div id="xhtml">XHTML</div>

<address>position style sheet test.
<b>position-2.htm</b> </address>
</body>
</html>
```

Notes:

1. See how the various words are superimposed. There is the standard heading level 3 containing: "Learn".

2. Then we have three division elements. Normally, these would appear one after the other in their own block space. But we have given the first division, identified with the attribute id="css", an *absolute* value. It has been absolutely positioned at:

Learn

CSS
&
XHTML

```
position:absolute;
top:80px; left:100px;
```

80 pixels from the top and 100 pixels from the left. We could use any of the length values (see page 133) for the `top` and `left` properties. But from the top and left of what?

In this instance, the division box is offset from the box which contains it. Can you work out what box contains the:

`<div id="css">` ?

It is the main `<body>` box. Therefore, the offset will be 80 pixels down from the top left corner and 100 pixels from the leftmost margin of the body box.

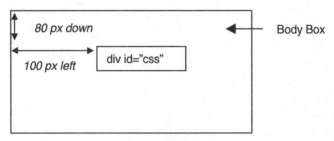

You could prove the above by setting the top property value to 8 pixels. 'CSS' now appears as follows:

LearnCSS

&XHTML

3. The second division, `id="and"`, the ampersand (&), has been positioned absolutely at:

```
position:absolute; top:95px; left:170px;
```

and the text colour is gray. We have used a character entity to display the ampersand, see Chapter 19.

4. Finally, the third division, `id="xhtml"`, has been positioned absolutely at 135px down and 210px left. The various block elements are thus overlapping.

5. We have also positioned the `address` element to be absolutely positioned at 200 pixels down to avoid it invading any of the `<div>` elements space.

Before looking at a few more examples, we shall look at the `position` and box offset properties (`top`, `right`, etc.) in detail.

position	
Value	`static|relative|absolute` `|fixed|inherit`
Initial	`static`
Applies to:	`all elements`
Inherited	`no`
Percentage	`not available`
Netscape & IE	`mainly implemented in both`

static: the box element (really its content) is laid out in the normal way. Thus all elements are `static` unless otherwise contradicted.

absolute: the element is considered to be a 'free agent' separate from the rest of the document. Such elements are positioned using the box offset properties and become independent of any other element. (This is why the address element had to be absolutely positioned, otherwise, its contents would appear underneath the heading with the absolute free agents floating around in the same area.)

relative: the element flows inline as normal, but it can then be positioned or moved relative to this natural position. See page 195 for an example.

Box Offset properties

top right bottom left	
Value	`length|%|auto|inherit`
Initial	`auto`
Applies to:	`positioned elements`
Inherited	`no`
Percentage	`refers to height of containing block`
Netscape & IE	`mainly implemented in both`

Usually, when an element is positioned we need to state its offset, i.e. where it will appear on the web screen. We may also want to use the `width` property to confine its width (and, indeed its height) to a particular area of the screen.

The `top, right, bottom` and `left` properties state where the element is to be placed. The values are the same as for those properties previously discussed. Try experimenting with these to see how they work.

Creating Columns without using Tables
Let us combine the `position, offset` and `width` properties to see how to create columns without resorting to tables.

189

Heading 3

Usually, when an element is postioned we want to state its offset, i.e. where it will appear on the web screen. We may also want to use the width property to confine its width (and, indeed its height).

The top, right, bottom and left properties state where the element is to be placed in relation to the relevant edge.

Fred Jones

Susan Hamshire

George Michaelis

Groucho Marx

position style sheet test. **3-cols.htm**

```
<html ..etc  >
<head>
<title>3-Columns</title>
<style type="text/css">
body      {font-family:arial, sans-serif;
           color:teal; font-size:10pt;}
h3        {position:absolute; top:0in;}
#column1  {position:absolute; top:2em;
           left:0.1in;
           width:1.2in; text-align:justify;}
#column2  {position:absolute; top:2em;
           left:1.5in;
           width:1.2in; text-align:justify;}
#column3  {position:absolute; top:2em;
           left:2.9in;
           width:1.2in; color:red;
           font:9pt/20pt;} /* 20pt line spacing */

address   {position:absolute; top:2.5in;
           left:0.1in;}
</style>
</head>
```

```
<body>
<h3>Heading 3</h3>
<div id="column1">
Usually, when an element is positioned we
want to state its offset, i.e. where it will
appear on the web screen. We may also want to
use the width property to confine its width
(and, indeed its height).
</div>
<div id="column2">
<img src="court.gif"
     alt="A courtyard." /> <br />
The top, right, bottom and left properties
state where the element is to be placed in
relation to the relevant edge. </div>
<div id="column3">
Fred Jones <br />
Susan Hamshire<br />
George Michaelis<br />
Groucho Marx<br />
</div>
<address>position style sheet test.
         <b>3-cols.htm</b> </address>
</body>
</html>
```

This works in IE5, not in Netscape. Netscape can position text, but has problems with positioning images.

Notes:

1. It would be worth studying this carefully. The important things to note are the absolute positions of the three columns and the heading and address. If the latter two are not also positioned, they will overlap the column text.

2. `column-3` uses the `font:9pt/20pt;` shorthand for a 9pt font-size and line-height (spacing) of 20pt.

3. Note too the way of incorporating comments in style sheets. `/* comment on one line */`

191

Creating a Drop Shadow

CSS2 allows a `text-shadow` property which is not implemented in either of the main browsers. However, we can achieve the effect in both Netscape and IE5 using the `z-index` property. We shall look at this first and then see how it can be used to create a shadow.

`z-index` property

In CSS2, each box has a position in three dimensions. In addition to their horizontal and vertical positions, a box also has a z-axis by which box elements can be stacked one on top of another. The default value is *automatic*, and this was used implicitly to overlap the words in Figure 15.1 on page 186. The order in which the text was stacked was the order in which they were encountered in the source code - *CSS, &, XHTML*. Because *XHTML* came last it was placed on top of the pile. But, another order can be imposed via the `z-index` property using the *integer* value.

z-index	
Value	`auto│integer│inherit`
Initial	`auto`
Applies to:	`positioned elements`
Inherited	`no`
Percentage	`not available`
Netscape & IE	`implemented in both`

integer: this takes values from zero upwards. Zero is the bottom of the pile. The element with the largest integer value will be placed at the top of the pile.

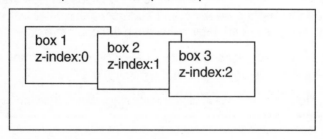

Here is an example using four image maps.

Maps: click the map for Norway

```
<html xmlns="http://www.w3.org/1999/xhtml"
xml:lang="en" lang="en">
<head>
<title>z-index with four images</title>
<style type="text/css">
h1      {font-family:arial, sans-serif;
         font-size:14pt;}
#image1 {z-index=0; position:absolute;
         top:50px; left: 0px;}
#image2 {z-index=1; position:absolute;
         top:100px; left: 50px; }
#image3 {z-index=2; position:absolute;
         top:150px; left: 100px;}
#image4 {z-index=3; position:absolute;
         top:200px; left: 150px;}
</style>
</head>
<body>
<h1>Maps: <span style="font-size:9pt;">click
the map for Norway </span></h1>
```

```
<img id="image1" src= "new-zea.gif" alt="New
Zealand" />
<img id="image2" src= "EU.gif" alt="European
Union" />
<img id="image3" src= "Norway.gif"
alt="Norway" />
<img id="image4" src= "Greece.gif"
alt="Greece" />
</body>
</html>
```

Note:

They overlap in the order in which they appear in the
source code. But, rather than re-ordering them in the
source code, you could now reverse their order simply by
changing the z-index integer values. Try it out.

*Netscape 4 has a problem with the positioning of
images. So the above works only in IE5.*

By using JavaScript, one of the maps could be clicked to
bring it to the front.

Using z-index to create a shadow effect

Before style sheets came to be used, an author would have
had to create the text (Party) and its shadows using
PhotoShop, for example, and then save it as an image file.
Then add an `align= "right"` attribute to position the
image so that the rest of the text would flow on the left, or
create a one row table with two cells. But with CSS, we can
create a drop shadow using the `z-index` property.

Come to my PARTY

```
<style type="text/css">
span      {font-size:30pt;}
#text     {position:absolute; left:250px;
           top:10px; z-index:2; color:black;}
#shadow1 {position:absolute; left:256px;
           top:12px; z-index:1; color:gray;}
#shadow2 {position:absolute;  left:260px;
           top:14px; z-index:0; color:silver;}
h1        {color: red; background:pink;}
</style>
</head>
<body>
<h1>Come to my </h1>
<span id="shadow1">PARTY </span>
<span id="shadow2">PARTY </span>
<span id="text">PARTY </span>
```

Nesting an Absolute in a Relative

As a final example, we show how an absolutely positioned element can be nested inside a relatively positioned paragraph.

The absolute positioned phrase ("The Queen") will flow from the top-left corner of the relative element. Wherever the relative element is positioned, its absolute element will travel with it. This works with both main browsers.

```
<style type="text/css">
p    {font-size:12pt; position:relative;
      top:0in; left:3em;width:3in; }
span {font-size:24pt; color:red;
      position:absolute; top:0px; left:10px;}
```

195

```
</style>
</head>

<body>
<h3>Relative with an Absolute</h3>
<p>Here is a piece of text, positioned
relative to the Web Page.
<span>The QUEEN</span> is positioned
absolutely within the paragraph.
</p>
<address>rel-abs-2.htm</address>
</body>
</html>
```

It is important to try out the various permutations for yourself. We have shown a few possibilities, but the permutations are numerous. The end effect is limited only by the imagination of the web page author.

visibility property

Elements may be hidden or made visible via the visibility property. Its main use is with JavaScript whereby readers can click the mouse to reveal or hide images or text. However, we shall mention it here so that those familiar with JavaScript can use it.

visibility	
Value	visible│hidden│inherit
Initial	inherit
Applies to:	all elements
Inherited	no
Percentage	not available
Netscape & IE	implemented in both

This property affects whether the box generated by an element is displayed or not.

visible: the generated box containing the element's content is visible.

hidden: the generated box containing the element's content is invisible - but still affects layout. In other words, the element is still in the document taking up its rightful space, but will not be seen. To suppress the space generated by the element, set the `display` property to `none` - see below. The element will then be invisible, and will not take up space on the screen.

If you want to hide something, why not simply omit it altogether? Well, JavaScript can be used to change the values of the `visibility` and the `display` properties to create dynamic effects. An element could then be made visible or hidden as a mouse moves over and out of the element's box.

inherit: inherits the visibility of its parent element. Thus, any children within the parent box will inherit the parent's visibility, unless, the children are given their own visibility.

The following CSS code makes the inline span text "The Queen" visible but the paragraph text block invisible:

```
p     {font-size:12pt; position:relative;
       top:0in; left:3em;
       width:3in; visibility:hidden; }
span {font-size:24pt; position:absolute;
       top:0px; left:10px;
       visibility:visible; }
```

With JavaScript, it should be possible to make the underlying paragraph text visible when a user moves the mouse over the phrase "The Queen". However, the CSS2 Specification does not specify the layout behaviour when values for these properties are changed by program-scripts. So there will be different interpretations by browsers.

`display` property

In a standard XHTML document, there is no real need to use this CSS property since the selector to which the display property is applied has a default display of its own.

Thus, a paragraph selector (`<p>`) is already assumed to be a block element and will be displayed as such. Likewise, a list selector, a table selector, a table row selector, (`li`, `table`, `tr`), etc., have built in displays. The `<em>`, the `<b>`, the `<i>` selectors are all displayed as inline elements.

The `display` property is really used with non-XHTML languages where a tag has to be given some display characteristic before it can have styles applied to it. XML, for example, allows authors to create their own tags, `<mytag>` ... `</mytag>`. MathML - the Maths Markup Language - can be embedded in an XHTML document when equations are required. If tags from either of these languages had to be displayed in bold and red on the Web by a browser, a display property would have to be given before any styles could be applied, thus:

```
mytag {display:inline;
      font-weight:bolder; color:red;}
```

display	

Value	`inline|block|list-item|run-in`
	`|compact|marker|table`
	`|inline-table|table-row-group`
	`|table-header-group`
	`|table-footer-group`
	`|table-row`
	`|table-column-group`
	`|table-column|table-cell`
	`|table-caption|none|inherit`

Initial	`inline`
Applies to:	`all elements`
Inherited	`no`
Percentage	`not available`

Netscape & IE	`not implemented for XHTML`
	`IE5 implements it for XML`
	`documents`

For a full description of this property for use with documents other than XHTML, refer to the W3C CSS2 specification at:

`http://www.w3.org/TR/REC-CSS2/visuren.html`

and see also, Chapter 21, page 275. However, some of the `display` values may prove useful when the browsers get around to implementing them. Here at least is the theory.

```
<?xml version="1.0" encoding="UTF-8"?>
<!DOCTYPE html
      PUBLIC "-//W3C//DTD XHTML 1.0
Transitional//EN"
"http://www.w3.org/TR/xhtml1/DTD/
    xhtml1-transitional.dtd">
<html xmlns="http://www.w3.org/1999/
      xhtml" xml:lang="en" lang="en">
<head>
<title>A run-in exercise</title>
<style type="text/css">
  h3 { display: run-in; color:red; }
</style>
</head>
<body>
<h3>A run-in heading.</h3>
<p>And a paragraph of text that follows it.
One day it may be implemented by all
browsers. </p>
</body>
</html>
```

This should produce:

A run in heading. And a paragraph of text that follows it. One day it may be implemented by all browsers.

Notes:

In the above example, we have asked for the `<h3>` selector to be displayed as a *run-in*. That means that if a block box follows a run-in box, the run-in box becomes the first inline box of the block box. Thus, the heading should be treated as being a part of the paragraph block.

```
<?xml version="1.0" encoding="UTF-8"?>
<!DOCTYPE html
      PUBLIC "-//W3C//DTD XHTML 1.0
      Transitional//EN"
"http://www.w3.org/TR/xhtml1/DTD/
```

```
xhtml1-transitional.dtd">
<html xmlns="http://www.w3.org/1999/
    xhtml" xml:lang="en" lang="en">
<head>
<title>Display compact exercise</title>
<style type="text/css">
    dt { display: compact; color:teal; }
    dd {margin-left:4em;}
  </style>
</head>
<body>
 <dl>
  <dt>A short DT </dt>
   <dd>and a description of short DT. </dd>
  <dt>A longer and longer DL </dt>
   <dd>and a description of longer DT. </dd>
 </dl>
</body>
</html>
```

This should produce:

A short DT	and a description of a short DT
A longer and longer DT	
	and a description of the longer DT

Notes:

Here we are setting the left margin of the <dd> to 4em and the <dt> to display as compact. Again, this should have the effect of being able to treat the dt block as a one line inline box, if there is sufficient room for the dd to be displayed on the same line. This can be done with the first, but not with the second dd because the second dt is too long. In this case, the contents of the dd is put on a separate line to avoid it overlapping the dt text.

What you have learnt

We have seen how to bring DTP features to our web pages using the positioning properties of CSS. We can overlap text and images, create newspaper columns without having to resort to tables, create drop shadows using the `z-index` property and how to make elements visible or hidden.

Test

1. Which are block elements and which are inline elements?

```
<em> <p> <div> <span> <body>
```

2. In the following, which box contains `<div>` and which contains `<p>`?

```
<body>
<div> some text ...<p>some paragraph text
...</p>
</div>
```

3. In the above code, the following style sheet applies:

```
p {margin-left:1in;}
div {margin-left:0.5in;}
body {margin-left:0.3in;}
```

Draw the containing boxes for all three.

4. In the following code, for the example on page 195,

```
<body>
<h3>Relative with an Absolute</h3>
<p>Here is a piece of text, positioned
relative to the Web Page.
<span>The QUEEN</span> is positioned
absolutely within the paragraph.
</p>
```

a) What would happen if the `<p>` element was set to `display:none`?

b) If the `<p>` element was set to: `visibility:hidden`

5. Why is the font shorthand written as `9pt/12pt` in the following:

```
p {font 9pt/12pt red;}    ?
```

6. Why was it necessary to position the address element in the example on page 190? Take off the rule and see what happens.

```
address {position:absolute; top:2.5in;
        left:0.1in;}
```

In the following, we combine both *absolute* positioning and *margin* settings.

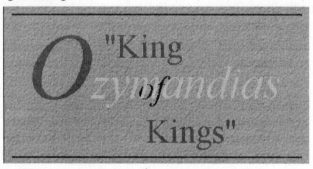

```
<style type="text/css">
body      {background-image:url("backcss.gif");}
span.oh   {font-size:200%; color:#a84500; }
div       {font-size:25pt; color:#286200; }
div.ozy   {position:absolute; top:0.2in;
           left:0.25in; font-size:35pt;
           color:silver; font-style:italic;}
div.king  {margin-top:0.2em; margin-left:1in;}
div.of    {margin-top:0.1em; margin-left:1.3in;
           color:black; font-style:italic;}
div.kings {margin-top:0.15em; margin-left:1.5in;}
hr        {color:black; }
</style></head>
<body><hr />
<div class="ozy">
<span class="oh">O</span>zymandias </div>
<div class="king">&#34;King </div>
<div class="of">of </div>
<div class="kings">Kings&#34; </div>
<hr /></body></html>
```

Part 3

Return to XHTML

In this final section, we shall return to XHTML to discuss:

Chapter 16: Forms

Chapter 17: Tables

Chapter 18: Image Hot Spots

Chapter 19: Character Entities

We then discuss how to validate (check for errors) our XHTML and CSS documents and then see what the connection is between XML and XHTML. We finish with some examples.

16: Forms

XHTML provides a means whereby information may be typed into a web page form by a reader, collected by the browser and sent off to some other location. In other words, you can solicit user input from your web page readers. Here are some instances where forms may be useful:

- registering for courses
- sending credit card details (!) for ordering goods
- forwarding abstracts of research papers for storage in a public database
- forwarding comments about the worthiness of some article to its author
- details for an on-line questionnaire
- soliciting information to be sent to a specific e-mail address
- typing in keywords for a *search engine*

The <form> tag is used in XHTML for getting readers to fill-in forms. The idea is to invite the user to type information into text boxes and/or click on various other boxes in the form. These boxes may be:

- blank text areas into which the user types in text
- clicking radio buttons, check boxes
- pop-up menus (for selecting items from a list)
- a submit button
- and usually a reset button.

When the submit button is clicked the data, which the user has entered, is collected together by the browser and sent off to its destination. The reset button clears any data entered by the user so that he or she may start again.

There is a problem. Each form has to have a program specifically designed to process the data. A web page with three forms would require three separate programs.

These form-programs may be written in any programming language, typically Java, C, C++; or, scripts (a Unix term for server programs) written in *perl, tcl*. It is beyond the scope of this text to delve into programming, and, in any case, writing such programs requires knowledge of the web server being used to process the data. However, there is one type of form submission which does *not* need any such programming knowledge. This is what we discuss in this Chapter. (For those who are interested, there is a brief discussion at the end of this Chapter, about the Common Gateway Interface (CGI) which is a standard mechanism for communication between *http* servers and the forms' programs, frequently called *gateway programs*.)

There is an example of a form in Fig 16.1 on page 209, where readers are invited to register for a JavaScript course. It could apply to many other applications such as ordering goods, tax returns, job applications, indeed any form which we may need to fill in.

How do we construct a form?

The entire form is enclosed within a pair of `<form>` tags. For the form to be of any use, it must also contain at least one empty `<input />` tag and, frequently, a non-empty `<textarea>` tag as well as a *submit* button so that the data can be sent off for processing.

```
<body>
. . . . . . . . .
<form method="post"
      action="mailto:myname@someplace">
<input attributes />
<textarea attributes> </textarea>
<input type="submit" />
</form>
. . . . . .  </body>
```

We shall discuss the `<form>` tag and its two main attributes before looking at the other tags. The form tag has a `method` and an `action` attribute.

The `method` attribute

The `method` attribute can take one of two values, either `get` or `post`. The `get` appends the data filled in by the user to the form-document's URL. It is called a *query* URL and consists of the form-document's URL, a question mark and the data itself.

You may have noticed this sort of thing in your browser's *Address* box *after* you have clicked on a *Search Engine's* search button. Here, I used *AskJeeves.com* to search for "Mack the Knife". The following is the data string sent to the server program:

```
http://askjeeves.com/main/askjeeves.asp?ask=Mack+
the+Knife&origin=&site_name=Jeeves&metasearch=yes
&IMAGE1.x=14&IMAGE1.y=11
```

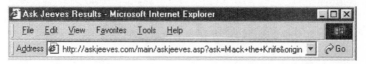

The `post` value (the one we need) can send the data either to a gateway program for processing, or to an e-mail address. But instead of being appended to the URL, the data is sent as a block. The default is the `get` value, but it can only send a limited amount of data and is not as secure as the `post` method.

The `action` attribute

Once the submit button is clicked, the data typed in by the user will be sent to the URL specified in the `action` value.[1]

---

[1] We now have three attributes which take a URL; the `href`, the `src` and here the `action`.

```
<form method="post"
action="http://www.abc.edu/cgi-bin/gateprog.xyz">
                         or:
<form method="post"
      action="mailto:fred@xyz.ac.uk">
```

The first example would send the data to `gateprog.xyz`
stored in the gateway programs' directory (`/cgi-bin/`) at
the web site `www.abc.edu` for processing.

The second example would send the data to the e-mail
address referenced in the `action` attribute, using the
`mailto:` protocol.

`<input />` - an empty tag

This tag specifies which type of display box to use within
the form. Each display box is automatically drawn by the
browser. It is an empty element and requires at least two
attributes: `type` and `name` and sometimes a `value`
attribute.

```
<input type="radio"
       name= "gender"
       value= "female" />
```

The `type` attribute

The value of the `type` attribute specifies which type of input
box to display in a form.

TYPE values	Purpose
"text"	for entry of typed text into a text box
"radio"	for the display of a radio button, usually, more than one is required
"checkbox"	for the display of checkbox(es)
"submit"	for the display of a submit button
"reset"	for the display of a reset button
"button"	for use with JavaScript

The `name` attribute

The `name` attribute's value, chosen (invented) by you, helps
to identify what data the user has typed when the e-mail

message is returned to the author. We shall examine several examples below and it will then make sense.

(For programmers: If the data is sent to a program, then the name attribute's value becomes a variable name.)

Register for Javascript Course

Please enter the following details:

	Firstname:
	Surname:
	e-mail address:

Previous Javascript Experience
⊙ None ○ Little ○ Fair amount

Have you:
☐ previous programming - *any language* - experience
☐ used Windows 2000 or NT
☐ used a Mac

Have you any specific requirements?
```
Enter specific
requirements here.
```

[submit details] [Reset]

Figure 16.1: A Course Registration Form

Here is the code which creates the form in Figure 16.1. We shall dissect it now in detail.

```
<?xml version="1.0" encoding="UTF-8"?>
<!DOCTYPE html PUBLIC "-//W3C//DTD XHTML 1.0
                       Transitional//EN"
"http://www.w3.org/TR/xhtml1/DTD/
        xhtml1-transitional.dtd">
<html xmlns="http://www.w3.org/1999/xhtml"
      xml:lang="en" lang="en">
<head>
<title>Registration for Javascript Course
</title>
<style type="text/css">
h2      {text-align:center; font-weight:bold;
         font-size:14pt; margin-bottom:0in;}
form    {margin-top:1em; font-size:9pt;
         color:red;}
div     {margin-top:1em;}
textarea {font-size:9pt; color:blue;}
</style>
</head>

<body>
<h2>Register for Javascript Course</h2>
<div>
Please enter the following details:
</div>
<form method="post"
      action="mailto:j.smith@abc.ac.uk">

<input type="text" name="firstname" size="20" />
Firstname:<br />
<input type="text" name="surname" size="20" />
Surname:
<br />
<input type="text" name="mailadd" size="20" />
e-mail address:
<div>
<b>Previous Javascript Experience</b>
<br />
<input type="radio" name="experience"
       value="none" checked="checked"/>None
<input type="radio" name="experience"
       value="little" />Little
```

```
<input type="radio" name="experience"
       value="famount" /> Fair amount
</div>
<div>
<b>Have you:</b> <br />
<input type="checkbox" name="prog"
       value="yes" />
previous programming - <i>any language</i> -
experience
<br />
<input type="checkbox" name="win2000"
  value="2000-nt" /> used Windows 2000 or NT
<br />
<input type="checkbox" name="mac" value="mac" />
used a Mac
</div>
<div>
<b>Have you any specific requirements?</b>
<br />
<textarea name="comments" rows="4"
cols="25">Enter specific requirements here.
</textarea>
<br />
</div>
<input type="submit" value="submit details" />
<input type="reset" />
</form>
</body>
</html>
```

Notes:
1. We have opted for the form's data to be e-mailed directly to the address given in the URL of the `action`'s value and, consequently, we need the `post` value for the `method` attribute.

```
<form  method="post"
       action="mailto:j.smith@abc.ac.uk">
```

If you wish the data to be handled by a program, perhaps to check credit card details against a data base, then someone will have to write a program. That person will have to tell you which `method` to use, the name of the

211

program and where it is held, so that you could supply the correct values for the `method` and `action` attributes.

2. The text box

```
<div>
<b>Please enter the following details: </b>
<form method="post"
      action="mailto:j.smith@abc.ac.uk">
<input type="text" name="firstname" size="20" />
Firstname:<br />
<input type="text" name="surname" size="20" />
Surname:
<br />
<input type="text" name="mailadd" size="20" />
e-mail address:
</div>
```

We have three text boxes, one for the firstname, a second for the surname and a third for an e-mail address. Since we want the box to precede the descriptive label, we have put the description after the `<input />` tag. The browser automatically creates the various input elements. We simply have to supply the type of element we need.

The `size` attribute

This simply specifies the *width* of the text box in characters. If the name typed in exceeds 20 characters, as specified by the `Firstname` text box, the extra characters will scroll horizontally in the box and *will be* included in the e-mail message.

The `name` attribute

Let us suppose that you have to prepare badge names for those attending the course. You want the first name followed by the surname: John Doe. How would you like it if the e-mail message sent back to your office machine simply gave the following two words: *Francis George*? Which is the firstname and which is the surname? (This implies that you have forgotten the placement of the boxes on the form - very easy if you have to deal with registrations for several courses at the same time, each one designed, perhaps, by different people.) *George Michael*, *Shelley Francis* are other obvious examples.

The `name` attribute solves the problem. What your e-mail message will display is the `name` attribute's value followed by an equal symbol followed by the data typed into the form, thus:

```
Firstname=Francis&Surname=George
```

Now, you cannot make a mistake! Each input element is separated from the next by an ampersand (&).

Note the use of the `<br />` tag when you want to force a display box onto a new line.

3. The radio button

We need to discover what experience of JavaScript, if any, course participants have. Radio buttons are ideal for this. The following would display three radio buttons (little circles which can be clicked).

```
<div>
<b>Previous Javascript Experience</b>
<br />
<input type="radio" name="experience"
        value="none" checked="checked"/>None
<input type="radio" name="experience"
        value="little" />Little
<input type="radio" name="experience"
        value="famount" /> Fair amount
</div>
```

Why is the `name` value the same in each case - *experience*? It tells the browser that the buttons with the same `name` value are a single group of mutually exclusive buttons and that only one is allowed to be clicked. If a reader clicks one and then decides to click another, the first one will automatically be deselected by the browser. Other examples are: *gender*. Male-Female; *rating*. Good-Average-Poor. Only one can be selected.

The `value` attribute

The value of the `value` attribute is attached to the value of the `name` value in the e-mail message: `experience=none`

If you think about it, the content of a text box can be anything (any surname, first name) but a radio button is chosen based on what the description next to it says. This description is just ordinary text entered by the author. It cannot be 'picked up' by the browser when the form is submitted. Consequently, *we* have to supply the text which will be submitted. Thus, in the example above, the e-mail message will contain one, and only one, of the following:

```
experience=none
experience=little
experience=famount
```

Note how the descriptive text is for the reader, but the `value` text is for the e-mail message, thus 'Fair Amount' has been shortened to `famount`. It is the author who chooses what he/she wants to see in the actual e-mail message and what should be displayed for the reader.

The `checked` attribute

This attribute simply puts a black dot on the radio button which has this attribute. We have put it on the first one. Note how it is written in XHTML: `checked="checked"`

> *My own personal opinion, take it or leave it, is never to add the* `checked` *attribute, simply because some readers will forget to make their selection for this part of the form and when they click on the submit button, the* checked *one will end up in your e-mail message even though the reader has not deliberately chosen it.*

4. The Checkbox button

```
<div> <b>Have you:</b>
<br />
```

```
<input type="checkbox" name="prog"
       value="yes" />
previous programming - <i>any language</i> -
experience
<br />
<input type="checkbox" name="win2000"
  value="2000-nt" /> used Windows 2000 or NT
<br />
<input type="checkbox" name="mac" value="mac" />
used a Mac
</div>
```

The checkboxes take the same attributes as the radio button. The `name`-value, however, needs to be different for each checkbox since *none*, *some* or *all* of the checkboxes may be selected.

Those which are not selected do not appear in the e-mail message, just those which have been selected. Thus, if programming experience and Mac were chosen, the e-mail message would read:

```
prog=yes
mac=mac
```

5. The `<textarea>` tag

```
<textarea name="comments" rows="4" cols="25">
enter specific requirements here. </textarea>
```

There is another text input field which is used when *multiple* lines of input are required, such as comments. This is done via the `<textarea>` tag, which unlike the `<input>` tag, requires a start and an end tag. Any text placed within the pair will appear in the textarea box.

Suppose we want our textarea box to have four rows (height) and 25 columns (width). The reader can type whatever they wish into this area. If the 'essay' exceeds the dimensions above, scroll bars will become active. The reader is not limited to 4 lines of 25 characters each in length. These are just the dimensions of the textarea box the author would like displayed on the web page.

My personal style again! I prefer not to enter text between the pair of `<textarea>` tags, since it requires action by the user to delete that text otherwise it will be included in the e-mail message along with whatever they did type in.

6. The `submit` & `reset` buttons

```
<input type="submit" value="Submit Details" />
<input type="reset" />
```

In the above, two buttons would be displayed. Clicking the submit button would send off the information to the URL defined in the `<form>` `action` attribute.

Browsers are programmed to take action whenever a submit button is clicked. They look at the form's `action` value to see where to send the data.

The `reset` button simply clears all the data which readers have entered so that they can start all over again, implying that they realise they have made mistakes.

Both buttons may take an optional `value` attribute. We have given one to the submit button. The value of the `value` attribute will appear on the button, not in the e-mail message.

In our case: *'Submit Details'* will appear on the submit button. The reset button has not been given a `value` and some default text would appear instead, such as *'Reset'*. 'S*end Query'* or *'Submit'* are typical default texts for the submit button when no `value` has been given.

Register for JavaScript Course

Please enter the following details:

Please enter your Firstname: `John`

Please enter your Surname: `Smith`

your e-mail address: `jsmith@acb.co.uk`

Previous JavaScript Experience ○ None ⦿ Little ○ Fair amount

The following details will prove useful to the Tutor:
Have you: previous programming - *any language* - experience ☑
used Windows 2000 or NT ☐ used a Mac ☑

Have you any specific requirements?

```
I need to know how to validate
forms using JavaScript & I am also
a vegetarian
```

[Submit Details] [Reset]

Figure 16.2

The e-mail message

Here is what would be sent to the author given the entries shown in Figure 16.2.

```
firstname=John&surname=Smith&mailadd=jsmith@ab
c.co.uk&experience=little&prog=yes&mac=mac&com
ments=I+need+to+know+how+to+validate+forms+usi
ng+JavaScript+%26+I+am+also+%0D%0A+a+vegetaria
n.
```

Each `name="value"` pair is separated by `&`. Spaces are replaced with the `+` symbol.

The message string sent as an e-mail is difficult to read and the person receiving the message would need to convert it into a more readable format.

I tend to copy and paste it into a word processor and then use a *Find/Replace* feature to find '+' and replace it with a *nonbreaking space* character. Likewise, I find all '&'s and replace them with the *manual line break*. I also recorded a macro to automate this task. Having selected the data string, I run the macro and the entire process is automated. Here is the result which is now much easier to read:

firstname=John
surname=Smith
mailadd=jsmith@abc.co.uk
experience=little
prog=yes
mac=mac
comments=I need to know how to validate forms
using JavaScript %26 I am also%0D%0A a vegetarian

But what are those strange things - %26 %0D %0A ?
They are ASCII characters typed in by the user in the textarea box but which cannot be printed by an e-mail program. It gives their equivalent hexadecimal number rather than the actual character. In the case of John Smith, he typed the following:

I need to know how to validate forms using JavaScript & I am
also *(Smith pressed the Enter key here)*
a vegetarian.

%26 is the ASCII code, in hexadecimal to represent the ampersand - &
%0D is the *Enter key*
%0A is a *line feed*

See Chapter 19 for more details about the ASCII character set. The % symbol is not part of the number, it is an e-mail indicator denoting an ASCII character which it cannot display.

So yes, a few strange characters will appear in your e-mail but you could always look up the ASCII character number and see what character the reader typed in.

Some e-mail programs display the form's data within the actual message box, others send the data as an *attachment*. So there will be variations between e-mail programs. You will need to find out what your particular e-mail program does.

Using Menus

In the following example, Figure 16.3, we show the use of a menu. Note the use of a drop-down arrow to reveal a list (a *menu*) of the courses on offer. The reader selects one and then clicks on the submit button.

Menus are used with many web pages when it is not convenient to show all the choices via checkboxes. You have probably noticed many examples already in web pages you have looked at, such as, a choice of domain names, what country you live in, what language would you like your web page in, your type of occupation, and so on.

A menu is created with the non-empty `<select>` tags and takes a `name` attribute.

```
<select name="course">
        <option selected="selected">
                HTML Level 1 </option>
        <option>  HTML Level 2 </option>
        <option>  CSS </option>
        <option>  DHTML </option>
</select>
```

Each item in the menu is contained in the `<option>` tag and the closing `</option>` tag. If the `selected` attribute is used that is the item displayed - *HTML Level 1* in the above.

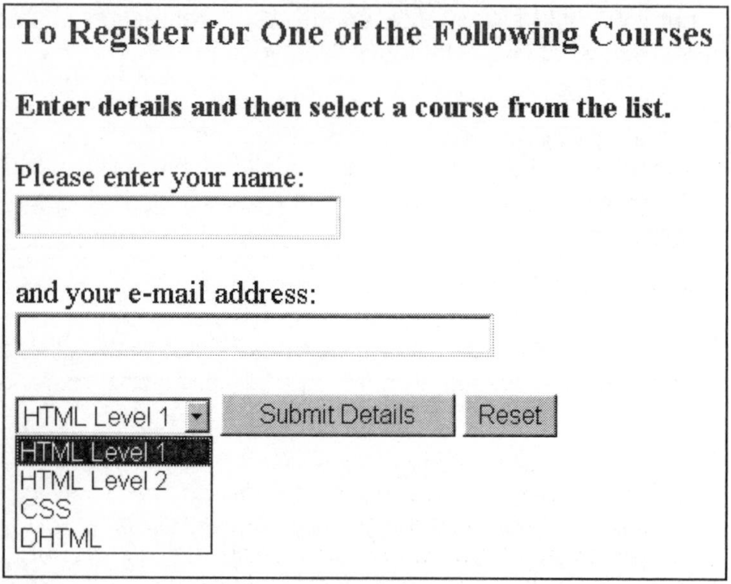

Figure 16.3

```
<body>
<h3>
To Register for One of the Following Courses
</h3>
<p><b>Enter details and then select a course from
the list.</b> </p>
<form method="post"
      action="mailto:j.shelley@ic.ac.uk">
Please enter your name:<br />
<input type="text" name="attendee" size="20" />
<br /> <br />
and your e-mail address: <br />
<input type="text" name="mailadd" size="30" />
<br /> <br />
```

```
<select name="course">
        <option selected="selected">
                   HTML Level 1 </option>
        <option>  HTML Level 2 </option>
        <option>  CSS </option>
        <option>  DHTML </option>
</select>
<br /> <br />
<input type="submit" value="Submit Details" />
<input type="reset" />
</form>
<hr /> </body> </html>
```

When the drop-down list arrow is clicked, the list of courses is displayed. The `<select>` tag's `name` value ("*course*" above) will apply only to the option selected by the user. Like radio buttons they are mutually exclusive. The one selected will appear in the e-mail message as - `course=CSS`

> **Warning:** *Do not use the <p> element within a form or around a <form>. The <form> and the <p> are blocks in their own right and seem to create conflicts. Browsers will accept them for the time being but the XHTML Validator will object most forcibly. Make use of one or more <br /> elements or the <div> element.*

Using the `multiple` attribute

There is a `multiple` attribute which if present allows the user to select multiple options rather like the checkbox buttons. When the attribute is not present, the user may select only one option as with radio buttons.

If the `size` attribute is present as well, see below, then this specifies the number of items to display, together with a scroll bar.

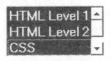

```
<select  name="course" size="3"
         multiple="multiple" >
```

There is one little problem when using the `multiple`
attribute. How do we select more than one choice? We
cannot simply click a second choice because this de-
selects the first choice!

On a Windows system, the trick is to make subsequent
choices by holding down the Control key and clicking
another choice. But what do Mac users do or, for that
matter, users of Internet home telephones, mobiles, TV-
desk tops, palm-tops, etc? Short of writing an essay
explaining what to do for every device, I would prefer not to
use multiple menus, but would resort to checkboxes. But
you must decide for yourself. Come to think of it, I have
never seen a multiple choice menu, though I have not
specifically searched the web looking for one.

However, if you do decide to make use of it, perhaps
because you are using it on an Intranet where you know
that everyone is using a particular operating system, how
does the data look in the e-mail message? Let us suppose
that someone has opted for CSS and DHTML. Here is what
will appear. Note how the same `name` value is attached to
each selection: `course=CSS&course=DHTML`

CGI

The Common Gateway Interface (CGI) is one of the
standard mechanisms for communication between web
servers and *gateway programs*. A *gateway program* is the
program specifically written to process the data sent from a
web page form.

When a web form is filled in and the user has clicked on the
submit button, the browser sends the data to the server site
where the processing program resides. That server will
then activate the program and pass it the data. Once the
data is processed by the program, it sends the results back
to the server which then passes it back to the web browser

and the user will receive the results, perhaps an acknowledgement of the receipt of some transaction.

Each server site has a special folder for storing these gateway programs, usually `/cgi-bin/`. As mentioned earlier, you can avoid using programs by having the data sent as an e-mail message directly to you.

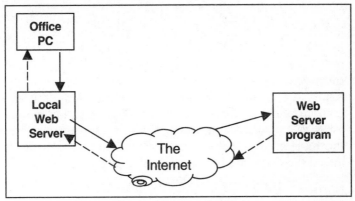

Figure 16.4
The Office browser is called the *Client*
The Web server holding the gateway program
is called the *Server* site

Incorrect Form Entry

What happens when a user does not fill in the boxes correctly? The gateway program would detect the error(s) and would have to send back messages to the Client browser to request re-entry of the information. This can take time and add to the amount of information (*traffic*) passing over the Internet.

One important development in web technology is the JavaScript programming language (see Chapter 21). This language can, amongst many other things, validate data entered - or not entered - by users. A program is written by the author of the web page and included along with the XHTML source code.

223

When the submit button is clicked, the JavaScript program-code (called a *script*) is automatically activated to check all the data and will submit the form only when it is correct. If it is incorrect, the script will notify the user and ask for the correct entries to be made.

This clearly reduces the amount of traffic as well as saving the user valuable connect time. This is what is known as *Client-side JavaScript*,[2] where the browser via the script can complete all the error checks before submitting the data to the Server-side for processing.

What we have learnt

We have seen how to create forms for data entry and how to submit them to our own office PC. The design of forms is not a trivial exercise as many of us know when we have had to fill in forms. Some are well laid out, others can be very confusing. One of the main principles of a web form is that it should not mimic a printed version.

Frequently, we need to translate a printed form on to a web screen. If we slavishly follow the printed version, we can end up with a dreadful looking Web form. It is far better to sit down and revise the complete design bearing in mind that it will have to be viewed on a screen.

Summary of XHTML Elements covered in Chapter 16

XHTML tag	Attributes	
`<form> ...` `</form>`	method action	get I post url
`<input />`	type name value size checked	text I radio I checkbox I submit I reset not required for submit or reset buttons not required for text box used with text box radio and checkboxes only

---

[2] See "Fun Web pages with JavaScript" by J. Shelley in this Babani series, BP 483. It teaches the JavaScript language through a series of practical examples.

XHTML tag	Attributes

`<select>`
`...`
`</select>`
	name
	multiple
	size

`<textarea>`
`...`
`</textarea>`
	name
	rows
	cols

`<option>`
`...`
`</option>`
	used with <select> for menu lists
	selected

Test

1. Why must the value of the `name` attribute be the same in the following:

```
<input type="radio"
       name="gender" value="male" /> Male
<input type="radio"
       name="gender" value="male" /> Female
```

2. What are the differences between an `input` element with `type="text"` and the `textarea` text box?

3. What is the danger in using the `checked` attribute on radio and checkbox buttons?

4. What purpose does the `value` attribute serve in a reset button and in a checkbox button?

17: Tables

The TABLE feature allowed HTML authors to do things which they could not otherwise do. For example, to create a two-column newspaper page, to put two or more images side by side on the same line, to have pretty bullet icons rather than the plain ones displayed by the browser. It is one of the 'design secrets' for many web pages. However, many of these features can now be done with style sheets, and without the overhead of the extra computing time the browser has to spend in laying out the table. Nevertheless, there are occasions when tables need to be used. So, here goes.

What is Covered
- `<table>` ..... `</table>`
- `<caption>` ... `</caption>`
- `<tr>` .... `</tr>`
- `<td>` .... `</td>`
- `<th>` .... `</th>`
- `<thead>` ..... `</thead>`
- `<tbody>` ..... `</tbody>`
- `<tfoot>` ..... `</tfoot>`

Tables & CSS
CSS2 added a number of properties for the table selector and is one of the major differences between the two versions. At the time of writing, neither of the main browsers implement the features fully, although IE5 has had a good attempt. Netscape does not implement properties for the following elements:

`<table>` `<thead>` `<tbody>` or `<tfoot>`

But it will accept a background property. ("Ah well, such is life!"): `table {background:red;}`

Many of the style sheet *font*, *text*, *margin* and *border* properties can be applied to `<td>`, `<th>`, `<thead>`, `<tbody>` and `<tfoot>` selectors. Clearly, too many to cover in detail here. Some examples are given in this Chapter, but you are advised to experiment with the numerous permutations, using both IE5 and Netscape so that you can see what works and what does not. However, by the time you read this text, some of the later versions of the browsers may have caught up with the CSS2 W3C Specification. If not, it is safer to stay with the XHTML attributes discussed in this Chapter.

The `<table>` tag

Figure 17.1 shows a simple table. Here is the code:

```
<body>
<h2>A Simple Table Example</h2>
<table border="1">
<tr>
<th> Header A </th> <th> Header B </th>
<th> Header C </th>
</tr>
<tr>
<td> Data 1 </td> <td> Data 2 </td>
<td> Data 3</td>
</tr>
<tr>
<td> Data 4 </td> <td> Data 5 </td>
<td> Data 6 </td>
</tr>
<tr>
<td> Data 7 </td> <td> Data 8 </td>
<td> Data 9 </td>
</tr>
</table>
</body>
</html>
```

A Simple Table Example		
Header A	**Header B**	**Header C**
Data 1	Data 2	Data 3
Data 4	Data 5	Data 6
Data 7	Data 8	Data 9

Figure 17.1

The entire table is enclosed in the non-empty pair - `<table>` ... `</table>` which can contain only two other tags: `<caption>` and `<tr>` (for a table row). If a `border` attribute is included in the `table` tag, lines will be drawn around the cells. The value of the `border` is an integer (a whole number) which represents the thickness in pixels of the border. See page 230 for more information.

The `<tr>..</tr>` tag

This non-empty tag defines one row in the table and contains two other elements - `<th>` (table heading) and/or `<td>` (table data). The first table row tag specifies how many cells that row contains. All subsequent rows *must* have the same number of cells as the first and each row must be terminated by the ending tag `</tr>`.

The `<th> .. </th>` & `<td> .. </td>` tags

`<th>` and `<td>` are used to specify what *data* appears in each cell. By default, browsers usually render the content of the `<th>` data centre-aligned and in bold. The data contained in a `<td>` cell is not bold and is left justified. However, both browsers allow style properties to be applied to the th and td selectors.

Yes, building a table is a chore. Each row and each cell and its data has to be typed in as you can see from the corresponding code for this example. I will mention a much faster way of doing it later.

The <th> and the <td> tags are non-empty. If either has no content then the corresponding cell is blank. The first row does not have to be a heading row with <th> tags, and it may appear anywhere within a table.

The <caption> tag

Each table can have an optional caption, which will centre its content across the table and, if necessary, wrap the text across the table as shown in Figure 17.2. The caption can contain text, images and hyperlinks. It is tempting to use a heading element rather than a caption element for tables. Resist the temptation! It is via the caption element that non-screen media can inform the user about the table's content. CSS allows for different positioning of the caption but this has not yet been implemented by either browser.

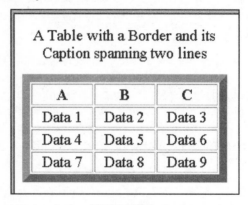

Figure 17.2

The border attribute

When present, the border attribute does two things. It adds grid lines to table cells and surrounds the table with a border. If the border is omitted or its value is set to zero, the table cells will have no grid lines and the table will not have a border. The value must be an *integer* number representing the thickness of the border in pixels. Adding a

230

`border-color` property (IE5 only) will set the colour for the border. Here is the code for Figure 17.2.

```
<style type="text/css">
table   {border-color:pink; color:teal; }
td      {text-align:center; color:black;}
caption {color:red; font-family:serif;}
</style>
</head>

<body> <center>
<table border="10" width="60%">
<caption>A Table with a Border and its
Caption spanning two lines
</caption>

<tr>
<th> A </th> <th> B </th> <th> C </th>
</tr>

<tr>
<td> Data 1 </td> <td> Data 2 </td>
<td> Data 3</td>
</tr>

<tr>
<td> Data 4 </td> <td> Data 5 </td>
<td> Data 6 </td>
</tr>

<tr>
<td> Data 7 </td> <td> Data 8 </td>
<td> Data 9 </td>
</tr>
</table>

</center>
</body> <html>
```

Notes:
`table {border-color:pink; color:teal; }`
The sad news is that Netscape does not implement style rules for the table element. However, one day ......! In the meanwhile, IE5 will give the border a pink colour and the table text will be in teal.

```
td     {text-align:center; color:black;}
```

All text data in `td` elements will be black and centre aligned in both IE and Netscape.

```
<table border="10" width="60%">
```

In both browsers, the border will create grid lines and a 10 pixel border around the table. Only IE5 will colour the border via the `color` property of the `table` selector.

The table has been given a width of 60%. When a % value is used, the table will always be 60% of the window, no matter what size the reader sets the window to. If a width of, say 350 pixels,

```
<table border="10" width="350px">
```

had been chosen by the author, then the table will always be 350 pixels, no matter what size window the reader chooses. Scroll bars will appear if the window is too small.

At the time of writing, neither of the main browsers fully implement style sheet properties for the table element. IE5 does much better than Netscape. The reason is that each browser has a different method for displaying tables. For the time being, it is safer to use in-line attributes for the table element.

CSS2 has added numerous styling properties for tables. Since many have not been fully implemented, it is difficult to provide examples. You are well advised to experiment with them in both of the main browsers to see which work and which do not. One way to overcome the problem, for the interim, is to use both style sheets and attributes. In general, style sheets declarations will override attribute styling. So you can at least get used to style sheets for the day when browsers catch up with the W3C Specification.

```
table {color:red; border:outset 0.2in green;}
```

In the above, IE5 would colour the table text in red; set a 0.2 inch thick border in green with an outset style.

We shall not cover CSS2 table styles in detail. It is left to you to check the full version in the W3C Specification.

IE5 implements all of the following and more. Netscape implements the `td` and the `caption`, provided the latter does not have to wrap the caption on to multiple lines. (Don't ask!) You can use many of the text and font properties on the `td` and `caption` tags.

```
<style type="text/css">
table   {color:black;
         background:url("watermark.gif"); }
td, th  {text-align:right;}
caption {background-color:teal;
         color:inherit;}
</style>
```

Some Effects Using Tables

Figure 17.3

By using the `rowspan` and `colspan` attributes within either `<th>` or `<td>`, we can specify the number of rows (vertical, deep) or columns (horizontal, across) the content should span. For example, Figure 17.3 was achieved using the code below:

233

```
<head>
<title>More Complex Table</title>
<style type="text/css">
table {width:50%; color:black;
        background-color:inherit;} /* stops CSS
                         Validator complaining! */
td {text-align:center;}
</style>
</head>
<body>    <table border="7">
<caption>Sales Data for 2001/02</caption>
<tr>
  <th rowspan="2">
<img src="geek-bird.gif" alt="The Geek" /> </th>
  <th colspan="2"> Sales </th>
</tr>

<tr>
   <td> 2001 </td> <td> 2002 </td>
</tr>

<tr>
   <td> Small cars </td> <td> 120,000 </td>
   <td> 150,000</td>
</tr>

<tr>
   <td> Big cars </td> <td>   </td>
   <td> 25,000 </td> </tr>
<tr>
  <td colspan="3">
    <b> Let's do Better in 2003.</b></td>
</tr>
</table>    ... etc. ...
```

Notes:

1. The Company's logo image spans 2 rows, (in depth), but takes up 1 column (across) and is, therefore, one cell across but two cells deep.

```
<tr>
  <th rowspan="2">
<img src="geek-bird.gif" alt="The Geek" /> </th>
  <th colspan="2"> Sales </th>
</tr>
```

"Sales" spans 2 columns and occupies two cells across but only one row deep. Therefore, the first table row specifies 3 cells in total. All other rows in the table must have the same number of cells.

2. In Row 2, "2001 and 2002" each occupy one column/cell. They can only go in columns 2 and 3 respectively of row 2. This is because the logo image already occupies the first column/cell of row 2 as stated in point 1 above. So there are only two cells left.

```
<tr>
   <td> 2001 </td> <td> 2002 </td>
</tr>
```

3. Row 3 is normal in that it has three cells and therefore three <td> tags.

```
<tr>
   <td> Small cars </td> <td> 120,000 </td>
   <td> 150,000</td>
</tr>
```

4. Row 4 also requires three cells but the middle cell is blank. (We did not make Big Cars in 2001.) We still need three <td> tags albeit with no content for the second <td>. Being highly suspicious of computer programs, I always like to give a <td> something to put in. In this case the no-break-space ( ) character entity. By doing this, you will also force the browser to add grid lines around the middle cell. Otherwise some browsers will not do so.

```
<tr>
   <td> Big cars </td> <td>   </td>
   <td> 25,000 </td>
</tr>
```

Row 5 has *a footer text* spanning 3 columns.

```
<tr>
   <td colspan=3> Let's do Better in 2003 </td>
</tr>
```

If you understand the above, you have mastered tables.

Why use Tables?

1. Inserting the image tag between <a> tags will make it a hyperlink image.

```
<tr>
 <th rowspan="2">
  <a href="somedoc.html">
   <img src="company_logo.gif" alt="Logo" />
  </a>
 </th>
 <th colspan="2"> Sales </th>
</tr>
```

2. The following will create a 'bulleted list' with the bullet being an image.

```
<center> <table>
<tr>
 <td width="10%">
  <img src = "mybullet.gif" alt="bullet image" />
 </td>
 <td width="80%">list item 1 text </td>
</tr>

<tr>
 <td width="10%">
  <img src = "mybullet.gif" alt="bullet image" />
 </td>
 <td width="80%"> list item 2 text </td>
</tr>
... etc ...
</table> </center>
```

Notice the use of the `width` attribute. This specifies the percentage of the row which one cell will occupy. In the above, we have a small image (the bullet) which takes up 10% of the entire row. The second cell will occupy another 80%.

What about the other 10%? How big is a table anyway? We should not ask this because it is not relevant. A table is sized according to how much text is contained in any given cell. In other words, it is the content in the cells, text or image, that governs the size of a table. However, by setting a `width` attribute in a `td` tag, an author can specify how big a cell and all the others in the same column should be.

By putting a `width` attribute on the *table* tag, an author can also specify how much of the entire screen the table will take up regardless of the amount of content. In this case, the browser will have to wrap text onto several lines within the cell if it cannot accommodate the data on one line. (Images, of course, cannot be wrapped so their physical width must be taken into account.) You should try using the `width` attribute on the `td` and `table` tags to verify the above. You will soon see how they work.

With a little imagination you can create some very pleasing effects with tables. You could try out the following to see what will result.

```
<table background="watermark.gif">
<table bgcolor="#ff5566">
<tr bgcolor="gray">
<td bgcolor="red">cell 1 </td>
<td bgcolor="pink">cell 2 </td>
```

Note the use of the `bgcolor` and `background` attributes which behave in the same way as for the `body` tag. Note, too, the spelling of the word 'gray' ('grey' comes out green! Why? See Chapter 21 where we talk about how browser programs take HTML errors into account.

background versus bgcolor

It is possible to have both attributes in the table and body tags.

```
<table background="watermark.gif"
       bgcolor="#443322">
```

So which will take precedence, the image or the colour? The image background will always sit over the coloured background. Should the image have any transparent areas, then the background colour will be able to shine through. (The behaviour is different with style declarations. It appears that the colour will take precedence.)

Text in Columns Using Tables

In HTML, tables were used to create columns of text. The trick is to create a table with one row and two cells. When the first cell is 'finished', add a second data cell, `<td>`, to create the second column. But we have already seen how to do this on page 190 without having the overhead of tables.

Using Tables for Layout - Design

Many web pages use tables to lay out their content rather than using them simply to present tabular data. Until cascading style sheets becomes more commonplace, page layout is achieved via tables. Here are three of the more popular 'designs' using tables.

Cascading style sheets enable even more interesting desk top publishing features and without the need of having to resort to tables.

1: Table Layout - 2 Columns	
link 1 link 2 link 3 ... etc. ... link n	This is really a two column table with two rows. The first row contains a Heading spanning two columns. - `<td colspan = "2">` The second row contains two `<td>` tags and a *width* attribute of, say, 20% in the first and 80% in the second. If the `border` attribute of `table` is not present, who is to know that a table is being used?

```
<table>
<tr> <td colspan="2">
<h1>1: Table Layout - 2 Columns </h1> </td>
</tr>
<tr>
<td width= "20%" valign="top">
<a href="url 1">link 1 </a> <br />
```

238

```
<a href="url 2">link 2 </a> <br />
etc... </td>
<td width="80%" valign="top"> This is really a
two column ... etc. ... </td>
</tr>
</table>
```

2: Table Layout - 3 Columns		
Links	As much text as you want can go here in the middle column of the second row.	Other related links or resources

3: Table Layout - 3 Columns again		
empty	As much text as you want can go here in the middle column of the second row. The two cells on either side of this middle cell are empty and will create white space, in effect putting in left and right margins.	empty

Cellpadding & Cellspacing

Cellspacing: This attribute allows for spacing between cells.

Cellpadding: This attribute allows for a padding between text and cell borders. You may well need to experiment with these two to convince yourself of their difference.

```
<table  border="7"  cellspacing="20">
```

`<table border="7" cellpadding="20">`

thead, tbody and tfoot elements

These three elements are not supported in Netscape. So why introduce them? Well, there are three reasons. The first is that when all browsers eventually support them, at least you will have come across them and will be able to use them effectively. The second reason is that they can be used as selectors and given styles accordingly.

But the main reason is if your web page has to be rendered on devices other than PCs then the heading columns can be repeated. For aural devices, the listener would be told which of the headings a body cell was referring to. For compact visual display devices, such as mobile phones and palm top computers, the header and the footer rows will be displayed all the time, with the body cells being scrolled within them. We must keep remembering that XHTML is destined to be used not just for PCs but for the many other types of Internet access devices.

Here is what the W3C Specification has to say:

> "tfoot must appear before tbody within a table definition so that user agents can render the foot before receiving all of the (potentially numerous) rows of data."

In this way, a non-PC device will be able to lay out the header and the footer and if necessary place the body of the table between scroll bars when the body cannot be completely displayed on a small screen device.

```
<table>
<thead>
  <tr>
    <th colspan="2"> header information </th>
  </tr>
</thead>
<tfoot>  <!-- Must precede tbody -->
 <tr>
   <td colspan="2">.footer information </tr>
 </tr>
</tfoot>
<tbody>
  <tr> <td> Data 1 <td> Data 2</td> </tr>
  <tr> <td> Data 3 <td> Data 4</td> </tr>
</tbody>
</table>
```

In the following example, we have given a `class` attribute (silver) to alternate rows so that the body rows can have alternate colours.

Head A	Head B	Head C
Data 1	Data 2	Data 3
Data 4	Data 5	Data 6
Data 7	Data 8	Data 9
Footer		

Warning: Since Netscape does not recognise `thead`, etc., these elements are ignored. Consequently, the `tfoot` row appears before the `tbody` rows.

241

```
<html xmlns="http://www.w3.org/1999/xhtml"
xml:lang="en" lang="en">
<head>
<title>Tables 3 CSS2</title>
<style type="text/css">
thead {color:red; text-align:center;}
tbody {color:green; text-align:right;}
tfoot {color:blue; text-align:center;}
tr.silver {background-color:silver;}
</style>
</head>

<body>
<table border="4">
<thead>
<tr>
<th>Head A</th> <th>Head B</th>
<th>Head C</th>
</tr>
</thead>

<tfoot>
<tr>
<td colspan="3">Footer </td>
</tr>
</tfoot>

<tbody>
<tr class="silver">
<td>Data 1</td> <td>Data 2</td>
<td>Data 3</td>
</tr>

<tr>
<td>Data 4</td> <td>Data 5</td>
<td>Data 6</td>
</tr>

<tr class="silver">
<td>Data 7</td> <td>Data 8</td>
<td>Data 9</td>
</tr>
</tbody>

</table>
</body>
</html>
```

What you have learnt

We have seen how to create tables and discussed some of the design effects when using them in web pages. It is worth experimenting with tables, especially with the various attributes the table tags can take. If you see a particularly good looking page, examine the source code and the chances are that tables have been employed to create the design.

We have also seen that not all elements can be used as CSS selectors, especially by Netscape. You will need to experiment to see which browser supports which selector and what style properties can be applied.

Summary of XHTML Elements covered in Chapter 17

XHTML tag	Attributes
`<table> .. </table>`	width - pixel or % values border bgcolor background cellpadding cellspacing
`<caption> .. </caption>`	none
`<tr> .. </tr>`	bgcolor

`<th> .. <th>`
  &
`<td> .. </td>`
	width - pixels or % values
	bgcolor
	colspan
	rowspan
	align
	valign

Test

1. How could you place three small images horizontally side by side?

2. Try this in IE and then in Netscape:

```
<table border="5" bgcolor="pink"
       cellpadding="10" cellspacing="10">
```
What did you observe?

3. How could you create this effect whereby the table has every other row shaded.

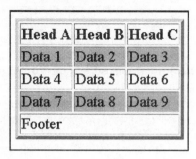

4. What is the difference between these two?
```
<table width = "50%">
<td width = "50%">
```

5. How would you get one cell coloured pink with the text in red?

6. How could you get a table to have a left border in one colour and the rest in white?

7. Which will work in Netscape 4.5?
```
table {background:red;}
table {background:url("watermark.gif";}
```

18: Image Hot spots

Hot Spots

A single image can have *hot spots* added so that when one of the spots is clicked, an `href` attribute in an `area` tag can be invoked. This feature is known as an *Image Map* because we create areas of hot spots on the image, just like a geographical map which has areas for regions, counties, countries, etc.

What we cover

- `<map>`
- `<area />`
- usemap
- shape
- coords
- how to work out the co-ordinates

An image map consists of three components:

1. the actual image itself which is linked to a `<map>` tag
2. the non-empty `<map>` tag which contains the areas to become the hot spots
3. the empty `<area />` tags which define each hot spot

Get the Image

This is an ordinary `<img />` element:

```
<img src="myimage.gif" alt="My Dog" />
```

except that we need to include a link to a *map* which is to be used to specify the hot spots. For this we need a new attribute for the `<img />` tag, namely: `usemap`.

```
<img src="myimage.gif" usemap="#mymap"
     id="fred" />
<map name="mymap">
.....
</map>
```

The usemap attribute of the `<img />` tag links the image to a non-empty `<map>` element whose `name` value is the same as the usemap value. The usemap value has a section marker (#) - just like that in an anchor tag's `name` attribute. `<a href="#venue">venue</a>`

The id attribute prevents the XHTML Validator from complaining. It likes to see it although it serves no purpose in our code. If it is not present, the Validator will produce an error and apologise for not being able to validate your document.

```
<map name="mymap" >
                  ^
Error: required attribute "id" not specified
Sorry, I can't validate this document.
```

The <map> & <area> tags

We shall now use these two new tags to create three hot spots in an image.

```
<img src="England.gif" alt="Map of England"
     usemap="#mymap" />
<map name="mymap" id="anyname">
<area href="mid-england.htm"
      alt="middle england"
      shape="rect"
      coords="175,68,231,95" />

<area href="south.jpg"
      alt="an excel spreadsheet example"
      shape="circle"
      coords="75,37,22" />

<area href="uk.gif"
      alt="enlarged map of the uk"
      shape="poly"
      coords="301,42,268,95,330,118,383,93,
              330,90,301,42" />
</map>
```

The non empty `<map>` element contains a number of empty `<area />` tags. Each one defines the position of the

246

hotspot in the image via its `coords` attribute. Do not be put off by all the numbers, they are very easy to work out!

The `shape` attribute defines one of three shapes: a circle, a rectangle or a polygon. Choose which shape best suits the area on the image which is to become the hot spot.

The `alt` attribute is used to provide text when a user points over a hot spot. Annoyingly, Netscape (version 4.5) does not show these `alt` values or when it does only one is shown. IE behaves in a more civilised manner.

The `href` attribute provides the URL of the file to be displayed when the hot spot is clicked. The file could be a larger image, a web page, an e-mail or newsgroup address.

> *The hot spot can also be used to execute JavaScript code. See Example 4 in Chapter 22.*

The `coords` attribute defines the area on the image which is to become the hot spot. This is done by entering pairs of *x,y* co-ordinates, each separated by a comma. The numbers must be in pixels and the actual number of pairs depends upon the shape of the area.

The 'difficult' thing is how to work out the co-ordinates. That is what we show below. There are little programs which can be used to create the XHTML for the `area` tag, but they have to be bought (or downloaded over the Internet) and then learnt. If you have an image processing program, such as PhotoShop, Image Composer, Photo Editor, Paint, it is easy to do it yourself. So why not?

Co-ordinates to create a rectangle:

Two pairs of co-ordinates are required. The upper-left X_1,Y_1 and the lower-right X_2,Y_2, that is four numbers in total, each separated by a comma.

Read off the ***pixel*** values from your image program. In PhotoShop jot down the *x,y* co-ordinates as shown in the *Information Window*. In Photo Editor, Image Composer and many other similar programs, the information is found on the *status bar line*. (See examples below.)

↖ X₁,Y₁

```
coords="x1,y1,x2,y2"
```

X₂,Y₂ ↘

Co-ordinates to create a Polygon:

You need to read off the *x,y* co-ordinates for each corner of the polygon:

corner 1: X(1), Y(1),
corner 2: X(2), Y(2),
corner 3: X(3), Y(3)
... etc.

This five sided polygon
requires 5 pairs, that is
10 numbers in total.

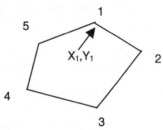

Co-ordinates to create a circle:

A circle is defined by its *centre* point - a single pair of *x,y* co-ordinates and its *radius*, resulting in three numbers.

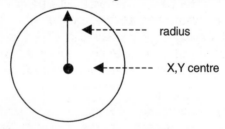

The radius is the distance from the centre point to the outer edge of the circle.

How to read co-ordinates from image programs

The following is a map of the Hawaii islands. We shall make three of the Islands hot spots.

Every image processing program will always show the x, y co-ordinates of where the cursor lies within the image. The trick is to know where to look for the values. You do not even have to be an experienced user of the program. You simply need to know how to open the image file and where to look for the co-ordinates.

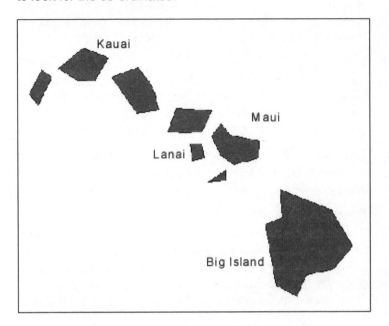

Circles - Adobe PhotoShop - Big Island

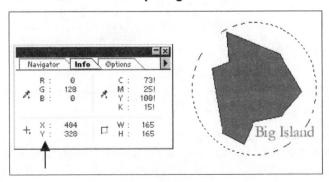

In PhotoShop 5, a simple way to select Big Island is to draw a circle around it, holding down the Shift key to draw a perfect circle. Make sure the `Info` palette is visible and then point your cursor in the centre of the circle and read off the x,y co-ordinates, 404, 328 in the above example.

Notice the WH (width / height), they should be the same for perfect circles: 165 in the above illustration. The radius will be half the height. $165/2 = 82.5$, say 82 pixels.

In the above, "`coords=404,328,82`" would define the co-ordinates for the circle. Although Big Island is an ideal polygon shape, I think a circle would be better for the user. Everything enclosed within the circle, including the surrounding sea will become the hot spot.

The same principle applies to all image processing programs. When a cursor is placed over a part of an image, the x,y co-ordinates are always shown *somewhere*.

Polygon - Photo Editor - Kauai

The next illustration is the polygon shape for Kauai Island. Note the cursor arrow is pointing at the top corner. Photo Editor displays the x,y co-ordinates in the bottom status bar after the cue word *Cursor*. Corner 1, then, is 96, 30. Repeat the process for each of the remaining four corners.

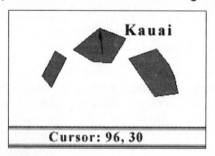

Rectangle - Image Composer - Lanai
Here is a rectangle for Lanai Island using Image Composer. The arrow points to the top-left corner and shows the *x,y*

co-ordinates for the first pair: 247,196. Incidentally, the WH shows the size in pixels of the entire image.

> **Tip:** *If you have made a selection, say by using one of the selection tools (ellipse, circle, rectangle, etc.), most image programs will give you the size of the selection as width and height values. This could prove useful if you need to work out the width and height values for an image to be displayed on your web page.*

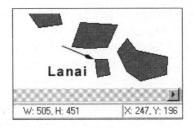

What you have learnt

We have seen how to create hot spot areas on an image so that when one is clicked, the relevant `href`-url will be displayed. Using hot spots is a good way to create a contents list rather than using the `<ul>` tag. Here is a simple example to give you the basic idea. It is one image file including all the text.

Each song title is a *rectangular* hot spot which when clicked could display a new page with the lyrics of the song via the `href` attribute of the `area` tag.

> *By using JavaScript, the lyrics could be displayed to the right of the image thereby obviating the need to fetch them over the Internet. See Example 4 in Chapter 22.*

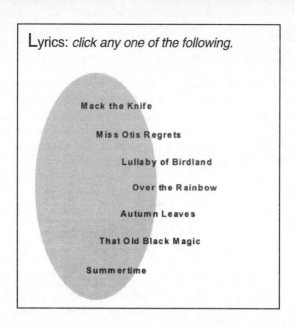

L yrics: *click any one of the following.*

Mack the Knife

Miss Otis Regrets

Lullaby of Birdland

Over the Rainbow

Autumn Leaves

That Old Black Magic

Summertime

Summary of XHTML Elements covered in Chapter 18

XHTML tag	Attributes
`<img />`	usemap refers to the map with the hot-spots
`<map>...` `    </map>`	name="somename" the value associates this map with a particular image
`<area />`	href alt shape: poly l circle l rect coords

X-Y Co-ordinates

At school, we learnt that the 'x' value starts at zero and increases as we move to the right. Unlike school, the 'y' value starts at the top left and increases as we move down.

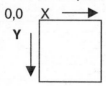

19: Character Entities

Character Entities

Some symbols, such as < > " & /, have a particular meaning when typed into XHTML source documents. If we want to display these characters, or other characters such as ½, ¼, we have to use *character entities*.

For example, should it be necessary to display:

"and <p> indicates the start of a new paragraph."

perhaps as part of a reference manual on XHTML, typing <p> as it stands would simply be interpreted by the browser as the start of a new paragraph. It, therefore, becomes necessary to use character entities for the *less than* (<) and *greater than* (>) symbols, as follows:

> and <**p**> indicates the start of a new paragraph.

A character entity begins with an ampersand symbol (&) immediately followed by the name of the entity and concludes with a semi-colon. A complete list of character entity names can be found later in this Chapter, but here are some commonly used ones:

Ch. Entity	Meaning	Symbol
&lt;	less than symbol	<
&gt;	greater than	>
&quot;	double quote mark	"
&amp;	ampersand	&
	no break space	*'a space'*
&#188;	one fourth fraction	¼
&#189;	half fraction	½
&#190;	three-fourths fraction	¾
&#225;	a acute	á

The last four have no names, indeed, very few character entities do have names. However, all of them have an ISO 8859-1 number. This number consists of a *hash* sign (#) followed by the *decimal* number of the character.

The no-break-space is particularly useful when you want additional spaces to be inserted between words, to indent text, etc. It is also the method by which you can ensure that multiple <br /> tags will take effect:


```
<head>
<title> character entities </title>
</head>
<body>
Here are two hash symbols:  -- &#35; &#35; <br />
The pound sterling &#163; symbol <br />
The word<strong>format</strong>
is in &lt;strong&gt; tags <br />
Try my Ros&#233; Wine.
</body>
```

Here are two hash symbols: -- # #
The pound sterling £ symbol
The word **format** is in <strong> tags
Try my Rosé Wine.

The ASCII Character Set

XHTML uses a basic character set ISO 8859/1, also known as Latin-1, based on an 8-bit alphabet. In fact, it is a sub-set of UTF-8 which is the character encoding system used by XML. It has over 40,000 characters and will have 100,000 in the future so that any language under the sun can be used. A sub-set of this, ISO 646, uses a 7-bit alphabet also known as ASCII, American Standard Code for Information Interchange. The Latin-1 set has 256 characters of which the first 128 characters are the ASCII character set.

In the following, the first 32 of the ASCII characters are special and are used to control printing and communication lines. These are not printable characters and only a few are shown. If you recall from Chapter 16 on Forms, our e-mail message included `%0A` and `%0D`. `A` is hexadecimal for decimal 10 and `D` for decimal 13. From the list below, we can now see these as referring to LF (line feed) and CR (carriage return).

In the following, no description is given when the meaning of the character is obvious. If a character has an *entity name* this is shown in the description. The name appears between an ampersand (&) and a semi-colon (;) for example, `&quot;`

Where names are not available, the ASCII decimal code number must be used preceded by a hash sign (#), thus, the tilde would be entered as a character entity as follows: `&#126;` Note that character entity names are lowercase sensitive!

Number	Character	Description
0	NUL	Null character
7	Bell	rings a bell
8	BS	backspace
9	HT	horizontal tab
10	LF	line feed
13	CR	carriage return
32		space character - * *
33	!	exclamation mark
34	"	*"*
35	#	hash sign
36	$	
37	%	
38	&	ampersand - *&*
39	'	apostrophe
40	(	
41	)	
42	*	

Number	Character	Description
43	+	
44	,	comma
45	-	hyphen
46	.	fullstop/period
47	/	solidus
48 - 57	0-9	digits 0 - 9
58	:	colon
59	;	semi-colon
60	<	&lt;
61	=	equals
62	>	&gt;
63	?	
64	@	commercial at
65-90	Letters A - Z	uppercase letters
91	[	
92	\	backslash
93	]	
94	^	caret
95	_	underscore
96	´	acute accent
97 - 122	letters a - z	lowercase letters
123	{	left curly bracket
124			vertical bar
125	}	right curly bracket
126	~	tilde
127	DEL	delete

For those who are interested in the various character sets employed in computers, try this site. It is one of the most comprehensive (34 pages) articles I have found. It abounds with further references. Before I read the article I did not realise just how complex is the process of representing characters in computers.

```
http://www.hut.fi/u/jkorpela/chars.html
```

For the rest of the Latin-1 character set, refer to the table on the next page. To find the decimal number for a character, use the first two digits in the left column and supply the third digit from the column headings. Thus, the yen symbol (¥) is read as 16 (row) & 5 (column), yielding the decimal number 165. Therefore, `&#165;` would give you a yen sign.

Latin-1 Characters from 120 - 259

	0	1	2	3	4	5	6	7	8	9
12	x	y	z	{	|	}	~		€	
13	‚	ƒ	„	…	†	‡	^	‰	Š	‹
14	Œ		Ž			'	'	"	"	•
15	–	—	~	™	š	>	œ		ž	Ÿ
16		¡	¢	£	¤	¥	¦	§	¨	©
17	ª	«	¬	–	®	¯	°	±	²	³
18	´	µ	¶	·	¸	¹	º	»	¼	½
19	¾	¿	À	Á	Â	Ã	Ä	Å	Æ	Ç
20	È	É	Ê	Ë	Ì	Í	Î	Ï	Ð	Ñ
21	Ò	Ó	Ô	Õ	Ö	×	Ø	Ù	Ú	Û
22	Ü	Ý	Þ	ß	à	á	â	ã	ä	å
23	æ	ç	è	é	ê	ë	ì	í	î	ï
24	ð	ñ	ò	ó	ô	õ	ö	÷	ø	ù
25	ú	û	ü	ý	þ	ÿ	Ā	ā	Ă	ă

Note the Euro symbol (128). As a character entity this would be typed as: `&#128;` It works in IE5 but it does not work with Netscape 4.5. However, both Netscape 4.5 and IE5 accept the following character entity name: `&euro;` which is easier to remember.

Your machine would need to have that character installed before it would print. Try the following site to download the € symbol:

```
http://www.microsoft.com/typography/faq/
                                 faq12.htm
```

The above address was current at the time of writing. If it fails, go to the Microsoft home page and type "euro symbol" in the search engine box.

20: Validating XHTML & CSS

Validating XHTML documents

You can check whether you have any errors in your XHTML document by using the W3C Validation Service. Create your page and save it on to your hard disc in the normal way. Let us say we have called it `maps.htm`.

Call up your browser and in the Address/Location box type in: `http://validator.w3.org/`

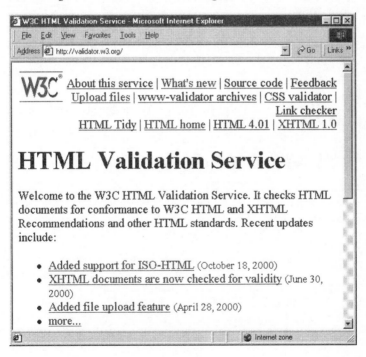

These screen shots are current at the time of writing. Hopefully, the site will remain even if the content changes at some future time.

Notice the second and third bullet. Clicking on either will display the following:

April 28, 2000:

> Added the <u>file upload</u> feature. (Thanks to Terje Bless for the patches!)
>
> Created the <u>www-validator-cvs mailing list</u>.
>
> Updated the <u>home page</u>, moved some things to <u>another page</u>.

Click on `Added the `<u>`file upload`</u>` feature` to display the following:

  Validator home | About this service | Feedback

HTML Validation Service

This form allows you upload files from your computer to have them validated.

File:

[   ] [Browse...]

☐ Show source input ☐ Show an outline of this document
☐ Show parse tree ☐ exclude attributes from the parse tree

[Validate this document] [Reset this form]

Click the Browse button. In the *Open file* dialogue box, locate the folder on your hard disc and then the XHTML file you wish to validate.

Then click the `Validate this document` button.

```
File:
D:\XHTML-CSS\TESTS\maps.htm                          Browse...
☐ Show source input ☐ Show an outline of this document
☐ Show parse tree   ☐ exclude attributes from the parse tree
    Validate this document          Reset this form
```

Your file now goes off to the W3C site. I was a bit dubious about this, thinking it may take some time. In practice, the results have always been returned very quickly, within seconds. This may be due to a number of things, such as having a copy on our local server. If you experience delays, it is possible to get proprietary programs to check your XHTML documents .

If you have errors, this is the sort of thing you will see. What errors are being pointed out? Notice the little arrows at the end of the line of source code. (I have changed the typeface and spacing, but the text is directly from the Validator.)

```
Line 24, column 35:
  <img id="image1" src= "new-zea.gif">
                                      ^
Error: required attribute "alt" not specified
Line 24, column 36:
  <img id="image1" src= "new-zea.gif">
                                       ^
Error: end tag for "img" omitted, but OMITTAG NO
was specified
```

The image tag has no `alt` attribute and does not have a forward slash to close it.

You can correct the errors and re-submit the file. When the document is eventually correct, you will see the Congratulations screen shown below.

W3C® HTML Validation Service Results

Document Checked

- File: D:\XHTML-CSS\TESTS\maps.htm
- Character encoding: unknown
- Document type: XHTML 1.0 Transitional with namespace http://www.w3.org/1999/xhtml

Below are the results of checking this document for XML well-formedness and validity.

```
No errors found! *
```

W3C XHTML 1.0 ✔ Congratulations, this document validates as XHTML 1.0 Transitional!

I find this service extremely useful and I highly recommend it. It is amazing what silly little things we do or do not do in our XHTML source code and this service helps to draw them to our attention. We must also remember, that many of the newer Internet devices will simply fall over if our XHTML is not 100% correct. So it is essential that we have a means of checking our source code, especially when coming from an HTML background where sloppy code was tolerated.

Validating CSS

We can also validate our style sheets, but to do so, we have to submit the style sheet as a separate file with a `.css` extension. Like the external style sheet, on page 109, it must not contain `<style>` tags.

Again go to : `http://validator.w3.org/`

W3C®   About this service | What's new | Source code | Feedback
Upload files | www-validator archives | CSS validator | Link checker
HTML Tidy | HTML home | HTML 4.01 | XHTML 1.0

Note the `CSS validator` link (third line above). Click on this to display:

W3C CSS Validation Service
Validate your cascading style sheet <u>by URI</u>
Validate your cascading style sheet <u>with a text area</u>
Validate your cascading style sheet source file <u>by upload</u>

Click on `by upload` and once the dialogue box on the next page is displayed, proceed as for XHTML.

The results are shown in a different way to the XHTML Validator. If there are no errors, it simply lists all the valid style rules and does not congratulate you. If you do have errors (and you have asked for *warnings* to boot) they will be listed along with the type of error.

The CSS Validator can be downloaded but you also need to install the Java interpreter. You normally have to type line commands to run the local copy of the validator program. I find that it is quicker to simply upload the file to the W3C site. However, you will need to experiment.

Validate your cascading style sheet

Enter the file name of the document you would like validated:

Upload a CSS source file

| | Browse... |

Warnings : No warnings ▼

| Submit this CSS file for validation | Reset this form |

Note how the `Warnings:` box contains `No warnings`. It is recommended that you click the small down arrow and select `All`. This will give a list all your errors and warnings.

> **Tip:** *To prevent the CSS Validator giving a warning message when the color property is used, always include the background-color property, and vice versa. Should you not want to provide an actual background colour, simply set the property value to transparent or, better still, inherit.*
>
> *Likewise, always make certain that you use one of the generic font family names when using the font-family property: serif, sans-serif, etc. See page 123.*

21: XML - XHTML - the Connection

HTML has had an enormous impact on how we use computers today. XML is said to be poised to have an even greater impact on tomorrow's computing. Should we be concerned?

Two current developments

The Internet, as opposed to the World Wide Web (for finding information), has become fashionable due, in no small measure, to HTML. It is set to become a major means of transferring and sharing information.

The second development is the new technology which has made possible many new devices capable of transferring information over the Internet - palm top computers, mobile phones, home telephone systems, TV boxes, talking car phones, etc. Some are small display devices, others are aural devices, some, like the TV boxes, cannot as yet scroll text. (Ever wished you could when reading Teletext?) Some computer analysts claim that by 2002 (others by 2005) 70% of Internet access will be via these devices rather than via our desk-top PCs.

If the above is true, then two things are needed. The first is to *standardise on data exchange*. But what language will be used? It cannot be HTML, it could not cope. So, a *new language* is required, the second requirement.

A Standard for Data Exchange

Let us take an example. Someone has a nasty accident and is taken unconscious to hospital. Ideally, the hospital will need that person's medical details from the GP and perhaps medical insurance details from an insurance company. The details will have to be entered into a hospital record for the patient.

Currently, the information will be in three different formats having been entered via some proprietary program. The GP will be using one program, the insurance company a second proprietary program and the hospital yet a third.

Eventually, the hospital will need to send back details to the GP and the insurance company. Again, someone will have to re-type the details into their own program.

Now, imagine if all three used the *same data format*. The data could now be sent over the Internet and simply dragged and dropped into the various local programs without any further human intervention (and the possible risk of incorrect typing). To do this would, of course, require some common or standard means of marking-up the original data which the three sites would have agreed to adopt. That is the sort of new language we need.

Sharing electronic information

Sharing electronic information has always been a problem and still is. How many times have you been unable to open an e-mail attachment? I use Excel but you send me a Lotus file. I send you a Word document but your version of Word is different. And what about the problem of data being held in different database programs. We seem to end up with something like this:

```
8BPS` ´ ` ` ` ` ` ` ` ` ~ ` ` ´ ` ` ´ ` ` ` ` ` ` ` ¯ 8BIM
~ é` ` ` ` ` x` ~ ` ` H` H` ` ` ` ^ Ú^ (ÿáÿâ^ ù^ F~ G˘ (¯ ü` ^
` ` ` H` H` ` ` ` ^ Ø^ ( ´ ` ` ` d` ` ` ` ` ~ ~ ~ ` ` 'ÿyyyyyyyy
ÿyyyyyyyyyyyy¨ è` ` ` ÿyyyyyyyyyyyyyyyyyyyÿ è` ` ` ÿyyyyÿ
ÿyyyyyyyyyyyyyyÿ è` 8BIM¯ ° ` ` ` ` ` Ł` ` ` ´ ` ` ^ @` ` ^
@` ` ` ` 8BIM¯ fl` ` ` ` H` ` HLino^ Ł` ` mntrRGB       XYZ
¨ Î^ ^ ` ` ` ` 1` ` acspMSFT` ` ` ` IEC
sRGB` ` ` ` ` ` ` ` ` ` ` ` öÖ¨ ´ ` ` ` ` Ó-HP
```

The data can seldom be imported without having to 'slap it around a bit'. To understand how to solve the problem, we need to go back to the Swinging 60s.

1960s

In the 1960s, it became possible to use computers for document processing. It then became clear that *content* and *structure* were two separate issues which had to be addressed when storing documents. Do you recognise the following?

> 21:XML - XHTML - the ConnectionHTML has had an enormous impact on why and how we use computers today. XML is said to be poised to have an even greater impact on tomorrow's computing. Should we be concerned?Two current developmentsThe Internet, as opposed to the World Wide Web (for finding information), has become fashionable due, in no small measure, to HTML. It is set to become a major means of transferring and sharing information.

It is first part of this chapter. It is the content without any structure. There are no line spaces before and after the paragraphs, no spacing before the headings. It is difficult to read. In fact, three concepts have been identified:

- *Content:*   A paragraph of text ....
- *Formatting - presentational - style* as in HTML

  ```
  <p>a <i> paragraph </i> of text. </p>
  <font color="red"> some text </font>
  ```

- *Descriptive information* - none in HTML apart from the <TITLE> tag

Latterly, people are becoming more concerned with how to *describe* content rather than just its style and structure.

The General Markup Language - GML

The first working system to address the first two concepts was the GML language devised at IBM in the late 1960s. It was used to produce their technical documentation. Managing and creating vast documents is not trivial.

Likewise, storing such data so that content and structure are preserved is not simple. Searching for and finding information is yet another problem.

For example, Boeing's 747 manual is some 150,000 pages. Suppose you need to find the specification of the bolt which holds on the engine. When many people are involved in writing the technical manual, some may name the bolt `bolt123`, another `123bolt`, others again `123-bolt`. It should be clear that some consistency in creating names needs to be enforced.

Jump 15 - 20 years to c.1984

By the 1980s, microtechnology had made its entrance and there was a proliferation of workstations used as local networks. There was a need to standardise the exchange of information between all the various network systems and their different operating systems. The American National Standards Institute (ANSI) had been established and had begun research into descriptive mark-up in 1978. The International Standards Organisation (ISO) joined the fray and produced the Standard General Markup Language (SGML) in 1984. It was based on IBM's GML.

Who uses SGML?

Large organisations which produce masses of documentation, such as the US Defense Department and the Association of American Publishers, could afford to introduce a single standard format for internal use. There were other requirements such as DocBook, for writing sets of books; the Text Encoding Initiative (TEI) for research, historical and lexicographical texts. Tim Berners-Lee turned to SGML when he wanted to develop a Web language.

What is SGML?

It is a meta language or template for defining other languages, such as TEI, MIL-STD (used by the Military) and HTML. It can be thought of as English grammar, a language used to write books and poems, or, say, the JavaScript programming language which is used to write short programs (scripts) for a Web page. Each language is different, thus TEI is not the same as HTML.

HTML

Tim Berners-Lee turned to SGML when he wanted to define a new language for Web browsers. But to understand SGML one has to be a guru. It requires extensive study, it is costly and it was overkill for creating web pages. Thus, HTML incorporated only the very simple features of SGML. More akin to the *Jack and Jill* children's reading books or comics rather than Milton's "Paradise Lost".

The design goals for HTML were:

- it should be easy to learn and use
- it should concentrate on content and structure
- it was intended for academic documents, containing textual information and some basic structure (lists, headings, paragraphs and blockquotes) but nothing fancy, just the odd bold and italic

It did not describe the content and was never intended to do so.

According to a myth, Tim Berners-Lee was surprised that the early HTML version did not catch on. However, when version 1 introduced images, HTML took off.

Since then, it has been hacked around. Forms, tables and frames have been added. The `<font>` tag allowed for text to have different typefaces and size as well as colour. Multimedia objects were included along with JavaScript and Java applets. Netscape and IE began to add their own variations and look what problems that caused!

The latest version is HTML 4 which supports cascading style sheets and JavaScript so that web pages can be changed when users click buttons or move their mouse over certain elements. This version is called Dynamic HTML (DHTML) by Microsoft.

HTML has done a wonderful job in promoting the widespread use of the Web. But it has become bloated with the many additions, some of which are not even HTML any more. It was originally designed to display text and to incorporate simple structure. It has had its day and will not be developed any further. It cannot cope with:

- the new devices
- the demands of e-commerce and m-commerce (for mobiles).
- with multimedia

The GIF image format is all right provided the image is not resized because then there will always be a loss of quality. Vector graphics are wanted. Search engines cannot really find exactly what we want because the content is not described. Browser programs have become far too big to take into account sloppy HTML source code. For example, what will a browser do with this?

```
<h2>A Heading </h4>
```

It is clearly wrong but most browsers will take some damage prevention exercise. Another example is the mis-typing of the colour `gray`. If `grey` is typed, many browsers will 'interpret' this as `green`.

Browsers will make a guess at what the author intended. But the extra code inflates the browser program. Large browser programs are fine for desk-top computers with their big RAMs and high speed processors, but the new smaller devices do not have the same memory capacity. Consequently, a new HTML is required which has a very strict syntax so that the program size can be reduced. But this also means that if the source code is not 100% correct, it will not work.

270

What does all this mean?

Let us return to our main point. We have two parallel requirements. First, a language which is capable of *describing* data so that information can be shared over the Internet. Secondly, a new HTML. Do we go back to SGML? No, it is too complex. What is needed is a new language which

- has 80% of the functionality of SGML but only 20% of its complexity
- is easy to learn and easy to use
- can describe its content

Enter XML.

XML

Here is an example of a pure XML document.

```
<?xml version="1.0"?>
<authorslist>
<author>
  <authorname>Fred Jones</authorname>
  <books>
    <book>
       <title>Balham - Gateway to the
                       South</title>
       <isbn>142-384-8675</isbn>
       <cost>£5.99</cost>
    </book>

    <book>
       <title>My Day out in Bootle</title>
       <isbn>142-384-8765-9</isbn>
       <cost>£7.99</cost>
    </book>
  </books>
  <hobbies>
    <hobby> Acol Bridge - level Master
    </hobby>
    <hobby> Wimbledon: seeded number 156
            in 1997
    </hobby>
  </hobbies>
</author>
```

```
<author>
  <authorname>Evelyn Waugh</authorname>
  <books>
    <book>Scoop</book>
    ... etc ....
</author>
</authorslist>
```

It describes the details about the books and hobbies of the authors Fred Jones and Evelyn Waugh. It is purely descriptive.

The above can be typed into any editor or word processor and saved as a text only file with an `.xml` extension. That is all there is to it.

Being a simple text file, it can now be opened in almost any program, NotePad, Word, Excel. I even 'opened' it in PowerPoint. It was still readable! It can also be read and understood by humans, just as it stands. So in the worst case, if this was sent over the Internet it could be opened in a word processor and read rather than the unreadable version on page 266.

Many programs we use today are being made XML compatible so that such files can be handled effortlessly.

Indeed, there is already one such program, Internet Explorer version 5. The screen shot on the next page is what the XML source code looked like when opened in IE5.

Note how IE5 shows minus and plus signs. By clicking on a minus, it collapses the contents, by clicking on a plus sign the contents are expanded. Another useful feature is that if you have any errors, IE5 highlights them and tells you what sort of error your source contains. But, if it displays the content, then your XML document is correct.

```
<?xml version="1.0" ?>
- <authorslist>
  - <author>
      <authorname>Fred Jones</authorname>
    - <books>
      ⊞ <book>
      - <book>
          <title>My Day out in Bootle</title>
          <isbn>142-384-8765-9</isbn>
          <cost>£7.99</cost>
        </book>
      </books>
    - <hobbies>
        <hobby>Acol Bridge - level Master</hobby>
        <hobby>Wimbledon: seeded number 156 in
          1997</hobby>
      </hobbies>
    </author>
  </authorslist>
```

Notes:

The first line, like our XHTML documents, contains:

<?xml version="1.0"?>

stating it to be an XML document. The entire document is encased in what is called a *root* element:

<authorslist> ... </authorslist>

Each author is contained within a pair of `<author>` tags. I invented all these names but they look like XHTML tags. additional authors can be added by anyone who can follow the basic pattern for Fred Jones.

Some tags are parent tags and contain children. IE5 marks these with the minus or plus signs. Those tags which do not have any children have no signs on them, such as `<title>` and `<cost>`. Tags may also take attributes, but this is not a book on how to create XML documents, so we shall not discuss them here.

Because our XHTML documents are XML documents, they too have a root element. Can you remember what it is? It is the `<html>` tags. The entire XHTML document is contained within this root element, see page 93.

Suppose, I am responsible for the travel books and a colleague of mine has responsibility for adding cookery book authors to this list. We would both have to use the same tags. This would be done by both of us agreeing on the names and order in which the tags are used, whether they have dependent children and whether the content is required, as with `<books>`, or optional as with `<hobbies>` perhaps we may not know the hobbies for some authors.

This is very easily done by creating another file called a Document Type Definition (DTD). This lists all the tags, their attributes if any, their children and the type of data they can contain.

As my colleague builds up a separate cookery file (it can be added to my list later), it can be verified against this DTD. Remember that our XHTML documents also have to be verified against a DTD - a list of all tag names, their attributes, etc. We have been using the transitional DTD in this text.

Learning XML is not difficult and if you know XHTML and its syntax, it will be even easier. (You may like to look out for my next book on XML.)

Because the basic document is a pure *text-only* file, it is very small and can travel over the Internet very quickly. Any program can read in this text file and if it is XML enabled, the tags can be interpreted. Excel 97, PowerPoint, Access have no difficulty reading the file just as it stands. Notepad or any word processor can also display it just as it stands. In the worst situation, if the file were my medical details, a human could at least read and understand the information. Many programs, such as those mentioned above, are currently being updated to become XML compatible.

IE5 is already XML compatible and that is why I was able to open the file in that browser. Furthermore, if I add just one more line to the above file, I could get IE5 to link to a style sheet and display it as a web page. Here is that extra line and the results of the web page.

```
<?xml:stylesheet href="authors.css"
                 type="text/css" ?>
```

The above has been displayed according to the following external style sheet authors.css:

```
book   {display:block;
        font-family: Arial, sans-serif;
        font-weight:bold; font-size: 12pt;
        color:silver;
        background-color:inherit;}
```

```
author {display:block;
        font-family: "Comic Sans MS",
        sans-serif;
        font-weight:bold; font-size: 11pt;
        color:teal;
        background-color:inherit;}

title {display:block;
        font-family: "Comic Sans MS",
        sans-serif;
        font-weight:bold; font-size: 10pt;
        color:black;
        background-color:inherit;}

isbn {display:inline;
        font-family: Arial, sans-serif;
        font-weight:200;
        font-style:italic; font-size: 10pt;
        color:green;
        background-color:inherit;}

cost {display:inline;
        font-family: Arial, sans-serif;
        font-weight:400;font-size: 10pt;
        color:blue;
        background-color:inherit;}

hobby {display:block;
        font-family: Arial, sans-serif;
        font-weight:bold; font-size: 9pt;
        color:teal;
        background-color:inherit;}
```

We mentioned the `display` property earlier in the book, on page 197. It does not play much of a role in XHTML, but it does for XML.

More about XML

XML is a meta language used for describing other languages but without the complexity of SGML There are quite a number of XML languages around, and growing all the time. There is XSL (the eXtensible style sheet language) which can be used as an alternative way of presenting XML languages and how to render content for the newer Internet devices. There is SVG (Scalable Vector Graphics) for improved image quality. SMIL (pronounced 'smile' Synchronized Multimedia Integration Language) for co-ordinating multi-media objects on web pages. There are MathML and ChemML, mathematical and chemical markup languages, for when mathematical and chemical notations are required. There is also XHTML.

All of these can be incorporated into other XML documents.

For example:

```
<?xml version="1.0" encoding="UTF-8"?>
<!DOCTYPE html
  PUBLIC "-//W3C//DTD XHTML 1.0
                        Transitional//EN"
  "http://www.w3.org/TR/xhtml1/DTD/
          xhtml1-transitional.dtd">
<html xmlns="http://www.w3.org/1999/xhtml"
      xml:lang="en" lang="en">
 <head> <title>A Math Example</title>
</head>
<body>
<p>The following is MathML markup:</p>
<math
xmlns="http://www.w3.org/1998/Math/MathML">
 <apply> <log/>
<logbase>
<cn> 3 </cn> </logbase>
<ci> x </ci>
</apply>
</math>
<hr />
</body>
</html>
```

In the above, some MathML source code has been inserted into the middle of an XHTML document.

XHTML

The new Web language is better suited for all the new Internet devices and has been defined according to XML not SGML. Therefore, it follows the syntax of XML. Basically this means creating well-formed documents, see page 84. New user agents will be able to render XHTML and other XML documents. Since XML and, therefore, XHTML has a strict syntax, the program code for the browsers will be smaller and more suitable for the new Internet devices.

As new members of the XML family are produced, these will become available to our XHTML documents.

New XML-compatible programs will come on the scene so that our data can be read with ease by many different programs.

We are in an interim period. Many large companies are already converting their existing HTML pages into XHTML and their data into XML. It is a large task.

You may like to explore HTML Tidy, a free program by courtesy of Dave Raggett. Originally, it was intended to tidy up sloppy HTML code but has now been extended to do much more, including converting HTML to XHTML. Try this site:

```
http://www.w3.org/people/raggett/tidy/
```

It is the beginning of the future. But for those who learn XHTML and CSS, they will be ready to take advantage of the coming tide.

> "There is a tide in the affairs of men,
>   Which taken at full flood, leads on to fortune;
>   Omitted, all the voyage of their life is
>   drowned in shallows and in miseries."

Brutus, Julius Caesar Act IV Sc. III

22: Some Examples

We shall look at some examples of style sheets to see how we can improve the appearance of our web pages. I am no expert in graphic design and am not suggesting that these are paradigms in any way. But they may give you some ideas. Follow through the source code especially for the style rules.

Example 1: Using margins and line spacing to add white space

Who we are - The Margin Makers

This is an example of using the margins to create white space on the Web page. It is easier to read and looks more attractive than what could be achieved without style sheets.

We have used a combination of the margin properties and the line-height property.

```
<?xml version="1.0" encoding="UTF-8"?>
<!DOCTYPE html
        PUBLIC "-//W3C//DTD XHTML 1.0
        Transitional//EN"
        "http://www.w3.org/TR/xhtml1/DTD/
        xhtml1-transitional.dtd">
<html xmlns="http://www.w3.org/1999/xhtml"
        xml:lang="en" lang="en">
<head>
<title>Adding white space</title>
<style type="text/css">
h1, p    {font-family:arial,sans-serif;
          font-size:11pt; }
h1       {text-align:left; margin-top:2%;
          margin-bottom:1%; margin-right:0%;
          color:#336666;
          background-color:inherit;}
p        {line-height:175%;
          text-align:center;
          margin-top:3%; margin-bottom:1%;
          margin-left:15%; margin-right:15%;}
p.notop {margin-top:3%;}
img      {margin-top:20pt;}
</style>
</head>

<body background="gray-3.gif">
<h1> Who we are - The Margin Makers</h1>
<p>
This is an example of using the margins to
create white space on the Web page. It is
easier to read and looks more attractive than
what could be achieved without style sheets.
</p>
<p>
We have used a combination of the margin
properties and the line-height property.</p>
<center>
<img src="cssimg-2.gif" alt="Snow Scene" />
</center>
</body>   </html>
```

This works for both Netscape 4 and IE5.

Example 2: A Warning Border & JavaScript

A warning

Red Alert!

Your Web server is on fire!

THE WARNING FLASHES IN DIFFERENT
COLOURS FOR 8 SECONDS.
But this code works only for Internet Explorer.

warning-2.htm

Here is the body of the document. The content is
uncluttered and easy to read. Note we have a `class` and
an `id` attribute.

```
<body>
<h1>A warning</h1>
<div class="warning">
<h2 id="warning1" >Red Alert!</h2>
<center>Your Web server is on fire!</center>
</div>
<p id="p23"> The Warning flashes in different
colours for 8 seconds.<br />
<span style="text-transform:none">
But this code works only for Internet
Explorer.</span>
</p>
<address><b>warning-2.htm</b> </address>
</body>
</html>
```

Here is the style sheet and the JavaScript code. If you are not familiar with JavaScript you can ignore the script code. It simply makes the phrase *Red Alert!* flash in different colours for 8 seconds in an attempt to draw the reader's attention to it. We stop it after a set period because it can become annoying.

```
<?xml version="1.0" encoding="UTF-8"?>
<!DOCTYPE html PUBLIC "-//W3C//DTD XHTML 1.0
                        Transitional//EN"
        "http://www.w3.org/TR/xhtml1/DTD/
         xhtml1-transitional.dtd">
<html xmlns="http://www.w3.org/1999/xhtml"
      xml:lang="en" lang="en">
<head>
<title>Warning</title>
<script type="text/javascript"
        language="JavaScript">
var colors=["red", "orange", "black",
            "FFFF00", "99CCCC"];
nextcolor = 0;
function changecolor(){
 document.all.warning1.style.color =
 colors[nextcolor++];
 nextcolor = nextcolor % colors.length;
} // EoFn

stopit=setInterval("changecolor()",500);
setInterval("clearInterval(stopit)",8500)
</script>

<style type="text/css">
h1, h2   {color:blue; font-style:italic}
.warning {font-weight:bold;
    background-color:#993344; color:#336666;
    margin-left:1in;  margin-right:1in;
    border-color: #99cccc;  border-width:4px;
    border-style:outset;}
.warning h2 {text-align:center;}
#p23         {text-align:center;
               text-transform:uppercase;}
</style>
</head>
```

Example 3: Overlapping text

Hopefully, you can make out the overall layout of the above screen dump.

```
<head><title> Wild Flowers </title>
<style type="text/css">
body {margin-left:0.55in; margin-right:0.5in;
      background:#ffcc99; color:inherit;}
div         {font-family:serif; }
div.wild    {color:#8a4500; font-size:35pt;
             background-color:silver;
             letter-spacing:1.25em;
             margin-left:0.1in;
             margin-right:3in; }
div.flowers {font-style:italic;
color:#286200; background-color:inherit;
        font-size:50pt; font-weight:bold;
        margin-top:-36pt; margin-left:0.2in;}
p.text {font-family:arial, sans-serif;
        letter-spacing:0.15em; font-size:9pt;
      color:#054400;background-color:inherit;
        font-weight:bold; margin-left:2in;}
.dropcap {font-size:300%}</style> </head>
```

```
<body >
<img src="flowers.gif" width="100"
    height="100" border="0" alt="Flowers" />
<div class="wild">wild</div>
<div class="flowers">
<span style="font-size:72pt;">f</span>lowers
</div>
<p class="text">
<span class="dropcap";
 style="color:#8a4500; float:left">S</span>o,
in this book, we shall be looking at the
programming and the client-side features of
javascript. We begin by assuming absolutely
no knowledge of JavaScript. but by the end of
the book, you will have learnt sufficient to
enable you to become competent web designers.
</p>
<address> wild-flowers-css.htm </address>
</body></html>
```

By the use of the margin properties, the main body of text
has been pushed over towards the right. The overlapping
texts have been constrained by the margin-right values.
Letter spacing does not work with Netscape.

Example 4: Filling blank holes

On the opposite page, we can see an empty space which is
filled with whatever menu is selected from the area hot-
spots. I have illustrated only the fourth menu with anything
significant. It can be seen on the page following. The
beauty of this is that we have neither had to resort to tables
nor to frames. JavaScript has been used so that when a
menu is clicked this triggers a function to display the
content referred to by the chosen hot spot.

You will be able to think up many examples for this kind of
design. It could be used for late-breaking news, for a variety
of short topics, lyrics of songs, etc. The amount of material
would have to be about the same length for each menu.

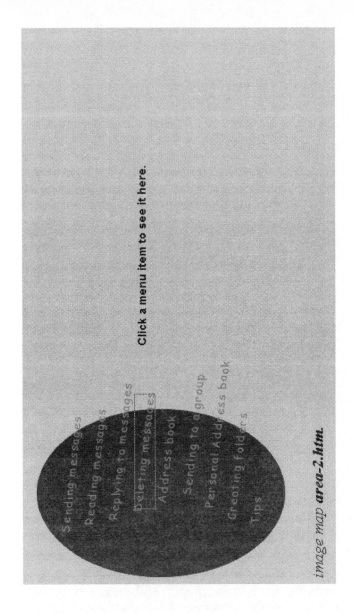

Click a menu item to see it here.

Sending messages
Reading messages
Replying to messages
Deleting messages
Address book
Sending to a group
Personal Address book
Creating folders
Tips

image map area-2.htm.

Past Times in Winter

"There has been a sea change in the way that the piple of this great country now see how the matter under discussion has progressed under this government. Despite what we inherited from the previous government, I now address Conference minded of the advances, in real terms, of resources ploughed into the current situation."
Deputy Prime Minister – 20th April, 2000

Sending messages
Reading messages
Replying to messages
Deleting messages
Address book
Sending to a group
Personal Address book
Creating folders
Tips

```
<?xml version="1.0" encoding="UTF-8"?>
<!DOCTYPE html PUBLIC "-//W3C//DTD XHTML 1.0
        Transitional//EN"
        "http://www.w3.org/TR/xhtml1/DTD/
        xhtml1-transitional.dtd">
<html xmlns="http://www.w3.org/1999/xhtml"
      xml:lang="en" lang="en">

<head>
<title> Hot-spots </title>
<script type="text/javascript" >
 oldtop = "div0";
function posn(x) {
newtop = x;
document.all(newtop).className = "divshow";
document.all(oldtop).className = "divhide";
oldtop = newtop;
} //EoFn
</script>

<script type="text/javascript">
var colors=["gray", "red", "orange",
"ffff00", "99cccc", "gray"];
nextcolor = 0;
function changecolor(){
document.all.warning1.style.color =
                        colors[nextcolor++];
 nextcolor = nextcolor % colors.length;
} // EoFn

stopit=setInterval("changecolor()",500);
setInterval("clearInterval(stopit)",8000)
</script>

<style type="text/css">
body {background-color:silver;
      color:inherit;}
.divhide, .divshow {position:absolute;
    top:100px; left:300px; color:red;
    background-color:inherit;}
div.divhide {visibility:hidden;}
div.divshow {visibility:visible;}
.divstart {position:absolute; top:200px;
           left:300px;}
```

287

```
h1, h2, h3 {font-family:sans-serif;
            color:#336666;
            background-color:inherit;}
h1.page1, h2.page1, h3.page1
            {text-align:right;}
p {color:#286200; background-color:inherit;
   font-family:arial, sans-serif;
   font-size:9pt;}
.warning {border-color:#99cccc;
   border-width:4pt; border-style:outset;}
</style>

</head>

<body>
<h1 style="font-size:14pt">
            Area - Hot Spots</h1>
<p id="warning1" class="warning"
    style=" position:absolute; left:350px;
            top:10px; font-size:11pt;">
You must use Internet Explorer 4 or
higher</p>

<img src="index-2.gif" usemap="#areas"
     border="0" alt="Index" />

<address>image map <b>area-2.htm</b>.
</address>
<map name="areas" id="map">
<area href="#stay1" alt="Index1"
      shape="rect"
      coords="60,39,199,65"
      onclick="posn('div1')" />

<area href="#stay2" alt="Index2"
      shape="rect"
      coords="69,71,210,96"
      onclick="posn('div2')" />

<area nohref="nohref" alt="Index3"
      shape="rect"
      coords="75,102,240,130"
      onclick="alert('Hallo Fred!')" />

<area href="#stay4" alt="Index4"
      shape="rect"
      coords="86,133,230,161"
      onclick="posn('div4')" /> </map>
```

```
<div id="div0" class="divstart">
 <p>Click a menu item to see it here.</p>
</div>

<div id="div1" class="divhide">
<p style=" color:red ">This is the text
relating to the division 1 paragraph. </p>
</div>

<div id="div2" class="divhide">
<p>This is the text relating to the division
2 paragraph. It will say a bit more than
division 1. </p>
</div>

<div id="div4" class="divhide">
<h1 class="page1"> Past Times in Winter</h1>
<img src="cssimg-2.gif"
     alt="Snow Scene" /> <br />  
<h2 class="page1">Coping with the Cold:
<br /> Old folks beat the snow </h2>
<h3 class="page1">by Bruegel,Pieter
<br />Netherlands Times, 1565</h3>
<div style="position:absolute; top:50px;
             left:200px; width:250px;">
<p style="color:#286200;
           text-indent:0.25in;">
"There has been a sea change in the way that
the piple of this great country now see how
the matter under discussion has progressed
under this government. Despite what we
inherited from the previous government, I now
address Conference minded of the advances, in
real terms, of resources ploughed into the
current situation." <br />
<font style="font-style:italic">
Deputy Prime Minister - 20th April,
2000</font>. </p>
</div>
</div>

</body>
</html>
```

Note the use of: `type="text/javascript"`

The `language` attribute is deprecated in favour of the `type` attribute. To maintain backward compatibility, I used both in the example on page 282.

```
<script type="text/javascript"
        language="JavaScript">
```

For those familiar with JavaScript, note how the usual `onClick` event handler is written in lowercase to satisfy the XHTML Validator.

Appendix A

Answers to Tests
References & Meta Tags

Test Chapter 2

1. *Create a basic template which you can use for all your XHTML documents.*

```
<?xml version="1.0" encoding="UTF-8"?>
<!DOCTYPE html
      PUBLIC "-//W3C//DTD XHTML 1.0
      Transitional//EN"
     "http://www.w3.org/TR/xhtml1/DTD/
      xhtml1-transitional.dtd">
<html xmlns="http://www.w3.org/1999/xhtml"
      xml:lang="en" lang="en">
<head>
<title>... template ...</title>
<style type="text/css">

</style>
</head>

<body>

</body>
</html>
```

2. *Is this correct XHTML?*

```
<p>Here is a paragraph with this word in
<B>bold</B> and this following text back to
normal. </p>
```

No. All tags must be in lowercase: <b> </b>

3. *Will your new XHTML files be displayed properly by those browsers which are only HTML compatible?*

Yes, because the HTML browsers will ignore references to XHTML. For example, the opening <html> will be recognised but the rest of the tag is simply ignored.

4. *What tag would you use to create a horizontal line across the whole width of the screen? Does this tag also have automatic spacing before and after the line?*

<hr />. It does have spacing.

5. *"The* <title> *tag puts a title on to your Web page." True or false?*

False. The title tag is used by the browser to put its content on the blue title bar, not the web page itself. You would need a heading tag within the body to do that.

6. *If you accidentally put in two sets of <body> tags into your Web page, what would a browser do?*

You cannot be sure. Some browsers would ignore the second tag. However, a strict XHTML browser should refuse to display the document. That is why you must use correct XHTML syntax.

7. *Which of the following tags are empty and which are non-empty tags: <head>
 <b> <title> <hr/> <h4> ?*

 and <hr/> are empty. The rest are non-empty.

8. *What is wrong with the following?*
<head>The ABC plc Home Page</HEAD>

There is no <title> tag. Remember that the <head> tags contains other tags, not text. If you do not have an opening and closing <title> element, the browser will not display the document. Finally, the closing </head> tag is not in lowercase.

9. *Why do we need a space after the tag identifier and the forward slash in empty tags:
?*

So that it will be recognised by HTML and XHTML browsers. An HTML browser will ignore the slash if there is a space before it.

10. *Suppose you have saved an XHTML file as text only, but have forgotten to change the file extension to .htm, saving it as fred.txt, for example. What will the browser display if you open the fred.txt file?*

It would display the file as a text only file, that is you would see only the source code. It is the htm extension which tells a browser that it is to open a web document and to display the content according to the mark up tags.

Test Chapter 3

1. *What is the difference between the `<p>` element and the `<blockquote>` element?*

Both have a line space before and after the content, but the blockquote will left indent its content.

2. *How many rules of XHTML syntax does the following break?*

```
<P>A paragraph of <b> bold text and <i> italic
</b> </i> text.
<div>Here is a division tag.<div>
```

Wrong case for P tag; the <p> tag is not closed; the closing </i> tag is incorrectly nested, it should come before the </b> tag; the <div> tag is not properly closed, it has no forward slash.

3. *What would happen if you ran the above code in a current browser?*

It works! Current PC browsers are tolerant of bad code. So why all the rules if we can break them? Simply because the newer Internet devices will display XHTML code only when it is 100% correct. In the future, many of your web pages may be accessed via the newer devices, consequently your code must be correct XHTML.

4. *How can you test whether you have written correct XHTML or not?*

Make use of the W3C Validator Service as described in Chapter 20.

5. *If a heading tag has an automatic line space after it and a paragraph tag has an automatic line space before, why would the following give only one line space between the two blocks and not two?*

```
<h1>A Level 1 Heading </h1>
<p> A paragraph of text ... </p>
```

Because of the rules for collapsing vertical white space as discussed on page 29.

Test Chapter 6

1. *How would you colour the background of your web page?*

Add the bgcolor attribute to the body tag: <body bgcolor="red"> or use a style rule as described in Part 2.

2. *When the* `bgcolor` *attribute goes for good, how will you be able to give a background colour to your web pages?*

Use a style rule as described in Part 2.

3. *Which attribute is used to reference a point within the same document?*

The name attribute in the <a> tag.

4. *How can you get your reader to send you an e-mail message without leaving the browser?*

Use the mailto: protocol in the href attribute of the anchor tag.

5. *You want a hypertext link to some other document but you have forgotten the URL, what can you do about it?*

It is pointless adding the href value unless you know the correct address. So, you will have to find the correct url or omit the link altogether.

Test Chapter 7

1. *What* `img` *attribute is required to display an image within a web page?*

The src attribute with a url as its value.

2. *If the image you want loaded is stored at some external site, what would happen if that site moved the image to some other folder without telling you?*

Tough luck! The browser would not find it. That is the danger when referencing other people's sites.

3. *Let us say that you see a web page with your organisation's logo on it. You would like to use it on your own web pages and have been given permission to do so. How would you obtain a copy of that logo?*

Simply right click the image logo and, from the pop-up menu, choose the Save Image As option. A dialogue box will open asking you where you want to save it and what name you want to call it. You may keep the original name if you wish to.

4. *You see a picture on someone else's web site and would like to use it for your own web page. The answer to the above question tells you how simple it is to obtain that image. But could you be in breach of copyright?*

Absolutely! You should always check for copyright. Some images are free and the owner will tell you. Otherwise, you should seek permission from the owner.

5. *You have made an image a hyperlink, but are now dismayed to find that a horrible blue line runs around the entire image box. It looks even worse after it is clicked because now the browser puts a purple border around the image. How can you get rid of the border?*

Simply add the border attribute with a value of 0:

<img src="url" border="0" />

6. *How can you tell whether you have Internet Assistant in your Word program?*

Click the File menu. If you see: Save As HTML, it has been installed.

7. *What is wrong with this?*

```
<img src=some.jpg>
```

Plenty. There is no alt attribute, now a requirement in XHTML; the tag is not closed and the quotes have been left off the src value.

Test Chapter 9

1. *Which of the following are valid ways of writing style rules?*

```
p
{
font-size:10pt; color:red;
}

p {font-size:10pt; color:red;}

p {font-size:10pt;
   color:red;}
```

All three. It is a matter of personal taste.

2. *How many errors can you spot in the following?*

a) H2 (fontfamily=maroon)
b) p {colour = "red";}

a) H2 is valid in CSS but not to be encouraged. The real howlers are: no hyphen between font and family; the correct property for colour is color; there should be a colon and not an equals sign to separate the property from its value; you must use curly brackets and not round brackets around style declarations. The semi-colon after a declaration is optional provided it is the only or the last declaration. But you are encouraged to always use the semi-colon.

b) The color property must be American spelling; again, colon not equals; values must not be quoted unless they contain white space.

CSS and XHTML are two different languages, each with its own syntax. CSS does not quote property values unless they contain white space, whereas in XHTML, all attribute values must be quoted. We need to learn (and remember) the syntax for each language.

Test Chapter 11

1. *Why will the W3C Validator give warning messages for the following style rules?*

I do not know! I could not find a reason in the W3C Specification. When you ask for warnings to be included in the Validation Service, see Chapter 20, this is what the service response is:

```
p {color:red;}
```
"You have no background-color with your color." (sic)

```
body {font-family:arial,helvetica;}
```
"You are encouraged to offer a generic family as a last alternative." (sic)

2. *Who are the parents and who are the children of the elements used in the following extract?*

```
<body>
<div> <p>some text <b>in bold</b> </p>
</div>
</body>
```

\<body> is the parent of \<div> (the child)
\<div> is the parent of \<p> (the child)
\<p> is the parent of \<b> (the child and childless)

3. *How can you get IE5 to show you the family tree for one of your XHTML documents?*

I would save the XHTML with an xml extension rather than the htm extension. Then open it in IE5 and it will be displayed as an XML file. (See Chapter 21 for further details.)

4. *What do the following length values mean?*

```
12pt   12px   12pc
```

12 points; 12 pixels; 12 picas.

5. *How many errors can you find in the following?*

```
<style>
h2 {font-style:small caps;
    font-size:12pts;
    text-colour:"teal': }
</style>
```

Eight: small-caps belongs to the font-variant property;
missing hyphen between small and caps;
points must be written without the s, 12pt;
there is no text-colour property, we must use color;
color must use the American spelling;
you cannot mix single and double quotes;
you cannot use quotes around values unless they contain white space;
a colon is not used to end a declaration.

I have done all the above and still do at times, that is why I am trying to help you.

6. *a) What font size will each of the paragraphs have, given the following source code?*

```
<style type="text/css">
p {font-size: 20pt; color:red;}
</style>
</head>
<body>
<p style="font-size:12pt">
First paragraph. </p>
<p> Second paragraph. </p>
```

The first <p> will be in 12 points because of the inline style which takes precedence over the style sheet.
The second <p> will be in 20 points because it is governed by the style sheet.

b) What will be the text colour contained in the first and the second paragraphs?

Both will be in red since they take the color style property from the style sheet.

7. *What is wrong with this?*

body {font:"comic sans ms", sans-serif, 12pt, red;}

In the font shorthand, commas must separate font-family typefaces, but other values must not be separated by commas. Also, red is not part of the font shorthand. It is always safer to put the font-size value as the first value. But do not ask me why!

Test Chapter 14

1. *You are surprised by the amount a heading (or paragraph, blockquote) text is indented. What factors will you take into account to adjust the amount of indentation?*

When using margins, borders and padding, all combine to indent text. Therefore, look carefully at your source code and work out what spacing you have given to each.

2. *What style rules would you use to create the following. Note how the horizontal rules are close to the heading.*

Margin Heading in Internet Explorer

Some text follows here ...

```
<style type="text/css">
h3 { margin-top:0in; margin-bottom:0in;}
</style>
```

3. *How would the browser window behave with each of the following?*

```
div {width:300px;}
div {width:80%;}
```

The 300px will keep the division at that size irrespective of the window size set by the user. The pixel unit is an absolute value. If the screen window is too small, scroll bars will appear.

In the second example, the division will always be 80% of whatever size window the user has set the browser window. It is a relative value.

4. *For the following style sheet:*

```
<style type="text/css">
body {color:rgb(0,0,255); line-height:16pt;
      font-family:helvetica, sans-serif;
      font-size:14pt; }
div.indent {margin-left:2em; margin-top:2em;
            color:#f00;}
</style>
<body>
<h1>Welcome to my Home Page </h1>
<div>Some welcome text ... </div>
<div class="indent">A special note follows
here ... </div>
</body>
```

a) What colour will the div.indent *text be in?* In red (#f00)
b) What colour will the <div> *text be in?* In blue.
c) What indentation will the <div> *text have?*
None. It is only the div with the class indent which will be indented.

Test Chapter 15

1. *Which are block elements and which are inline elements?*

<em> <p> <div> <span> <body>

<p>, <div> and <body> are block. The rest are inline.

2. *In the following, which box contains* <div> *and which contains* <p>*?*

```
<body>
<div> some text ...<p>some paragraph text
...</p>
</div>
```
The <body> box contains the <div>. The <p> will be contained in the <div> box.

3. *In the above code, the following style sheet applies:*

```
p {margin-left:1in;}
div {margin-left:0.5in;}
body {margin-left:0.3in;}
```

Draw the containing boxes for all three.

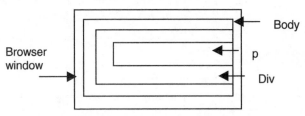

Note that the three boxes are left-indented only.

4. *In the following code, for the example on page 195,*

```
<body>
<h3>Relative with an Absolute</h3>
<p>Here is a piece of text, positioned
relative to the Web Page.
<span>The QUEEN</span> is positioned
absolutely within the paragraph.
</p>
```

a) What would happen if the <p> element was set to `display:none`?
It would not be visible *and* it would take up no space on the web page.

b) If the <p> element was set to: `visibility:hidden`
It would not be visible but it would take up its own space. If the span element were set to visibility:visible, its content would be visible but not the rest of the paragraph. This could generate some interesting effects when combined with JavaScript. Netscape does not recognise the visibility property.

5. *Why is the font shorthand written as* `9pt/12pt` *in the following:*

```
p {font 9pt/12pt red;}    ?
```

That is the CSS syntax. The first is taken to be the font size, the second to be the line height. CSS has to invent some means of distinguishing between the font-size and line-height point sizes in the font shorthand. It separates both with the forward slash and the first value is font size.

6. *Why was it necessary to position the address element in the example on page 190? Take off the rule and see what happens.*

```
address {position:absolute; top:2.5in;
         left:0.1in;}
```

If it were not positioned absolutely, it would appear with the other text. Remember that absolutely positioned elements are free floating elements.

Test Chapter 16

1. *Why must the value of the* `name` *attribute be the same in the following:*

```
<input type="radio"
       name="gender" value="male" /> Male
<input type="radio"
       name="gender" value="male" /> Female
```

To make them mutually exclusive.

2. *What are the differences between an* `input` *element with* `type="text"` *and the* `textarea` *text box?*

The first has one line allotted to it. The textarea box can contain multiple lines.

3. *What is the danger in using the* `checked` *attribute on radio and checkbox buttons?*

If the user forgets to check a box, the checked boxes will be sent off when the submit button is clicked as though the user had deliberately chosen them.

4. *What purpose does the* `value` *attribute serve in a reset button and in a checkbox button?*

On the reset button, it is the text which appear on the button. In a checkbox (and radio button) it is the text will be sent off when the submit button is clicked.

Test Chapter 17

1. *How could you place three small images horizontally side by side?*

Create a table with one row and three cells. Put each image in one cell.

2. *Try this in IE and then in Netscape:*

```
<table border="5" bgcolor="pink"
        cellpadding="10" cellspacing="10">
```

What did you observe?

The presentation is different. Netscape shows a white background. IE5, on the other hand, colours the background between the cells. (I prefer Netscape's presentation.)

3. *How could you create this effect whereby the table has every other row shaded?*

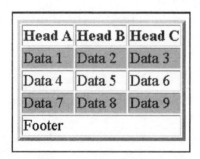

To make it work in both IE and Netscape, add a bgcolor attribute to each alternate row. Alternatively, you could add a class attribute to each alternate row and colour it using the background property.

```
tr.shade {background:teal;} .....
<tr class="shade">
```

4. *What is the difference between these two?*

```
<table width = "50%">
<td width = "50%">
```

The first fixes the size of the entire table at 50% of the user's window, The second sets the cell column at 50%. The other cell columns will take up the remaining space.

5. *How would you get one cell coloured pink with the text in red?*

Use a style rule for that cell, perhaps with an id attribute, and use the color property for the text, and a background property for the background colour.

6. *How could you get a table to have a left border in one colour and the rest in white?*

```
table {border-left-color:red;
       border-right-color:white;
       border-top-color:white;
       border-bottom-color:white;}
```

7. *Which will work in Netscape 4.5?*

table {background:red;} **Netscape yes!**
table {background:url("watermark.gif";} **No!**

References

These site addresses were valid in December 2000.
But sites do come and go.

HTML-tidy
http://www.w3.org/people/raggett/tidy/

W3C home page
http://www.w3.org/

CSS2 Specification
http://www.w3.org/TR/REC-CSS2/

CSS Validation Service
http://jigsaw.w3.org/css-validator/

XHTML Specification
http://www.w3.org/TR/xhtml1/

XHTML Validation Service
http://validator.w3.org/file-upload.html

Language Codes: Try this site for a complete set of the language codes:
http://www.w3.org/WAI/ER/IG/ert/iso639.htm

Character codes
http://www.hut.fi/u/jkorpela/chars.html

A Glossary of Typography
http://www.redsun.com/type/

€ symbol:
http://www.microsoft.com/typography/faq/
faq12.htm

XML Namespaces
http://www.xml.com/pub/a/1999/10/names/
namespaces.html

Using <title> & <meta> tags

Automatic programs called *web crawlers, spiders, robots* - amongst other terms - trawl the Web looking for keywords in Titles, Headings and URLs, and compile databases from them. Should you want your document to be included in these databases, add a <title> tag and a <meta> tag within the <head> of your document.

The title tag should contain keywords describing the content of the document. Long titles are seldom used. To add extra keywords which can be picked up by search engines, use the meta tag.

The <meta> tag

The meta tag is not a required tag when creating your web pages. But, if present, they can be used by search engines to list your page on their database index. You may need to register your page with one or more search engines before they will visit your site to see what your page is all about.

The meta tag should be placed after the title tag and usually takes the general form:

```
<meta name="somename" content="some content"
                                                     />
```

It is an empty tag and should not contain any line breaks. In other words, if the content part extends over the line, just keep typing and allow word wrap to take effect.

Here are two useful meta tags. The first provides a description, the second provides a list of keywords. This makes it easy for spiders to automatically index our web pages. The content for the description could be a word, a phrase or a paragraph. It should be kept reasonably brief.

```
<meta name = "description"
      content = "a brief description of your
page allowing word wrap if it extends over a
line." />
```

Choose whatever keywords you think might be appropriate, each must be separated by a comma.

```
<meta name="keywords"
      content="a, list, of, keywords, each,
separated, by, a, comma" />
```

Remember to include synonyms, Americanisms and so on. If you have a web page about cats, you could include pets, cat, kittens, even kitty. This is how I accidentally (really!) came across M/s Kitty's home page for those who wanted a spanking good time.

I have seen some keywords lasting almost a full A4 page! It deliberately included typing errors, mis-use of case and plurals. Many popular search engines are able to distinguish between these variations, so there is not the same need to go 'over the top' as in previous days.

Appendix B

Summary of CSS Properties & values

Property	Values
font-family	family name ⏐generic name
font-style	normal⏐italic⏐oblique
font-variant	normal⏐small-caps
font-weight	normal⏐bold⏐bolder ⏐lighter 100⏐200⏐300⏐400⏐500⏐600⏐ 700⏐800⏐900
font-size	absolute⏐relative ⏐length⏐%
font *shorthand*	for family, size, variant, weight and style
text-indent	length⏐%
text-align	left⏐center⏐right ⏐justify
text-decoration	none⏐underline⏐overline⏐ blink⏐line-through
text-transform	capitalize⏐uppercase ⏐lowercase⏐none
vertical-align	baseline⏐sub⏐super⏐top ⏐bottom⏐text-top ⏐text-bottom⏐middle⏐% ⏐length
line-height	normal⏐#⏐length⏐%
word-spacing	normal⏐length
letter-spacing	normal⏐length
color	color: rgb()⏐#rrggbb⏐#rgb ⏐colorname
background-color	color: rgb()⏐#rrggbb⏐#rgb ⏐colorname⏐transparent
background-image	uri⏐none
background-repeat	repeat⏐repeat-x ⏐repeat-y⏐no-repeat

Property	Values
background-position	%|length|top|center|bottom|left|right
background-attachment	scroll|fixed
background *shorthand*	for color, image, repeat, attachment, position
margin-top|right|bottom|left	length|%|auto
margin *shorthand*	[1-4] length|%|auto
padding-top|right|bottom|left	length|%|auto
padding *shorthand*	[1-4] length|%|auto
border-top|right|bottom|left-width	length|thick|thin|medium
border-width *shorthand*	[1-4] thick|thin|medium
border-top|right|bottom|left-color	color: rgb()|#rrggbb|#rgb|colorname
border-color *shorthand*	color|transparent
border-top|right|bottom|left-style	none|hidden|dotted|dashed|solid|double|groove|ridge|inset|outset
border-style *shorthand*	[1-4] none|hidden|dotted|dashed|solid|double|groove|ridge|inset|outset
border-top|right|bottom|left *shorthand*	for width, style, color
border *shorthand*	for width, style, color
float	left|right|none
position	static|relative|absolute|fixed
top|right|bottom|left	length|%|auto
z-index	auto|integer
visibility	visible|hidden

Property	Values
display	inline|block |list-item|run-in |compact|marker|table |inline-table |table-row-group |table-header-group |table-footer-group |table-row |table-column-group |table-column |table-cell |table-caption|none

Strict DTD

The following tags and attributes form part of the Strict DTD.

Element	Attributes
`<a>`	id, class, style, name, href, onfocus, onblur, title, shape, coords
`<abbr>`	id, class, style, title
`<acronym>`	id, class, style, title
`<address>`	id, class, style, title
`<area>`	id, class, style, title, shape, coords, href, nohref, alt (required), onfocus, onblur
`<b>`	id, class, style, title
`<base>`	href
`<big>`	id, class, style, title
`<blockquote>`	id, class, style, title
`<body>`	id, class, style, title, onload, onunload
` `	id, class, style, title
`<button>`	id, class, style, title, name, value, type, onfocus, onblur
`<caption>`	id, class, style, title
`<cite>`	id, class, style, title
`<dd>`	id, class, style, title
`<del>`	id, class, style, title, datetime
`<div>`	id, class, style, title
`<dl>`	id, class, style, title
`<dt>`	id, class, style, title
`<em>`	id, class, style, title

Element	Attributes
`<form>`	`id, class, style, title, action` **(required)**`, method, onsubmit, onreset`
`<h1>...<h6>`	`id, class, style, title`
`<head>`	`required`
`<hr />`	`id, class, style, title`
`<html>`	`XHTML root element`
`<i>`	`id, class, style, title`
`<img>`	`id, class, style, title, usemap, src` **(required)**`, height, width`
`<input>`	`id, class, style, title, type, name, value, checked, size, src, alt, usemap, onfocus, onblur, onselect, onchange`
`<li>`	`id, class, style, title`
`<link>`	`id, class, style, title, href, type, rel, rev, media`
`<map>`	`id` **(required)**`, class, style, title, name, onclick, ondblclick, onmousedown, onmouseup, onmousemove, onmouseout, onkeypress, onkeydown, onkeyup`
`<ol>`	`id, class, style, title`
`<option>`	`id, class, style, title, value, selected`
`<p>`	`id, class, style, title`
`<pre>`	`id, class, style, title`
`<script>`	`type` **(required)**`, src`
`<select>`	`id, class, style, title, name, size, multiple, onfocus, onblur, onchange`
`<span>`	`id, class, style, title`
`<strong>`	`id, class, style, title`
`<style>`	`type` **(required)**`, media, title`
`<sub>`	`id, class, style, title`
`<sup>`	`id, class, style, title`
`<table>`	`id, class, width, border, cellspacing, cellpadding`
`<tbody>`	`id, class, style, title, align, valign`
`<td> & <th>`	`id, class, style, title, rowspan, colspan, align, valign`

Element	Attributes
`<textarea>`	`id, class, style, title, name, rows & cols` **(required)**`, onfocus, onblur, onchange, onselect`
`<tfoot>`	`id, class, style, title, align, valign`
`<thead>`	`id, class, style, title, align, valign`
`<title>`	`part of <head>`
`<tr>`	`id, class, style, title, align, valign`
`<ul>`	`id, class, style, title`

Here is a list of other tags in the Strict DTD which you may like to examine in an XHTML reference guide.

`<bdo>`	`<code>`
`<col>`	`<colgroup>`
`<dfn>`	`<fieldset>`
`<ins>`	`<kbd>`
`<label>`	`<legend>`
`<meta>`	`<noscript>`
`<object>`	`<optgroup>`
`<param>`	`<q>`
`<samp>`	`<small>`
`<tt>`	`<var>`

Summary of Transitional DTD

The Transitional DTD contains all the elements and attributes of the Strict DTD plus those listed below. Use of the following tags is to preserve backward compatibility with HTML but they are deprecated and may be removed from future versions of XHTML.

Element	Description
`<applet>`	used to include a Java applet in your Web page
`<basefont>`	used to define the base (i.e. default) font size
`<center>`	to centre text and images
`<dir>`	same as the <ul> tag
`<font>`	to change colour, size and face of text

Element	Description
`<menu>`	same as the `<ul>` tag
`<s>` and `<strike>`	to strike-through text
`<u>`	to underline text

The following tags are part of the Strict DTD, but we list those *attributes* which do not form part of the Strict DTD. For example, in the Strict DTD, the `<br />` tag takes the following attributes: `id`, `class`, `style` and `title`. The `clear` attribute is not part of the Strict DTD but is supported in the Transitional DTD.

Element	Attributes
`<a>`	`target`
`<area>`	`target`
`<base>`	`target`
`<body>`	`background, bgcolor, text, link, vlink, alink`
` `	`clear`
`<caption>`	`align`
`<div>`	`align`
`<dl>`	`compact`
`<form>`	`target`
`<h1>...<h6>`	`align`
`<hr />`	`align, noshade, size, width`
`<img>`	`name, align, border, hspace, vspace`
`<input>`	`align`
`<li>`	`type, value`
`<link>`	`target`
`<ol>`	`compact`
`<p>`	`align`
`<pre>`	`width`
`<script>`	`language`
`<table>`	`align, bgcolor`
`<td> & <th>`	`nowrap, bgcolor, width, height`
`<tr>`	`bgcolor`
`<ul>`	`type, compact`

Frameset DTD

This is identical to the Transitional DTD except for these two elements for use with frames.

`<frame> & <frameset>`

Index

Note that 'f' stands for 'and following pages'

Notes: